AF521615

# The Cat

First published 2021 by order of the Tate Trustees by Tate Publishing, a division of Tate Enterprises Ltd, Millbank, London SW1P 4RG

www.tate.org.uk/publishing



A catalogue record for this book is available from the British Library

ISBN 978-1-84976-738-5

Project Editor: Emma Poulter
Production: Roanne Marner
Picture Researcher: Emma O'Neill
Design: Joe Ewart
Colour reproduction by DL Imaging, London
Printed and bound in Italy by Printer Trento S.r.l.

The author
Emilia Will is an editor at Tate and a freelance author. Interested in the intersection of fine art, popular culture, politics and folklore, she lives in South London where she spends her spare time growing things.

Cover:
Felicitas Vogler *Photograph of Ben Nicholson holding his cat, Tommy* 1968.
See p.33

Overleaf:
Duncan Grant *Girl at the Piano* 1940.
See p.89

# The Cat

Emilia Will

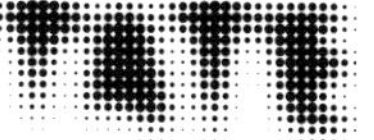

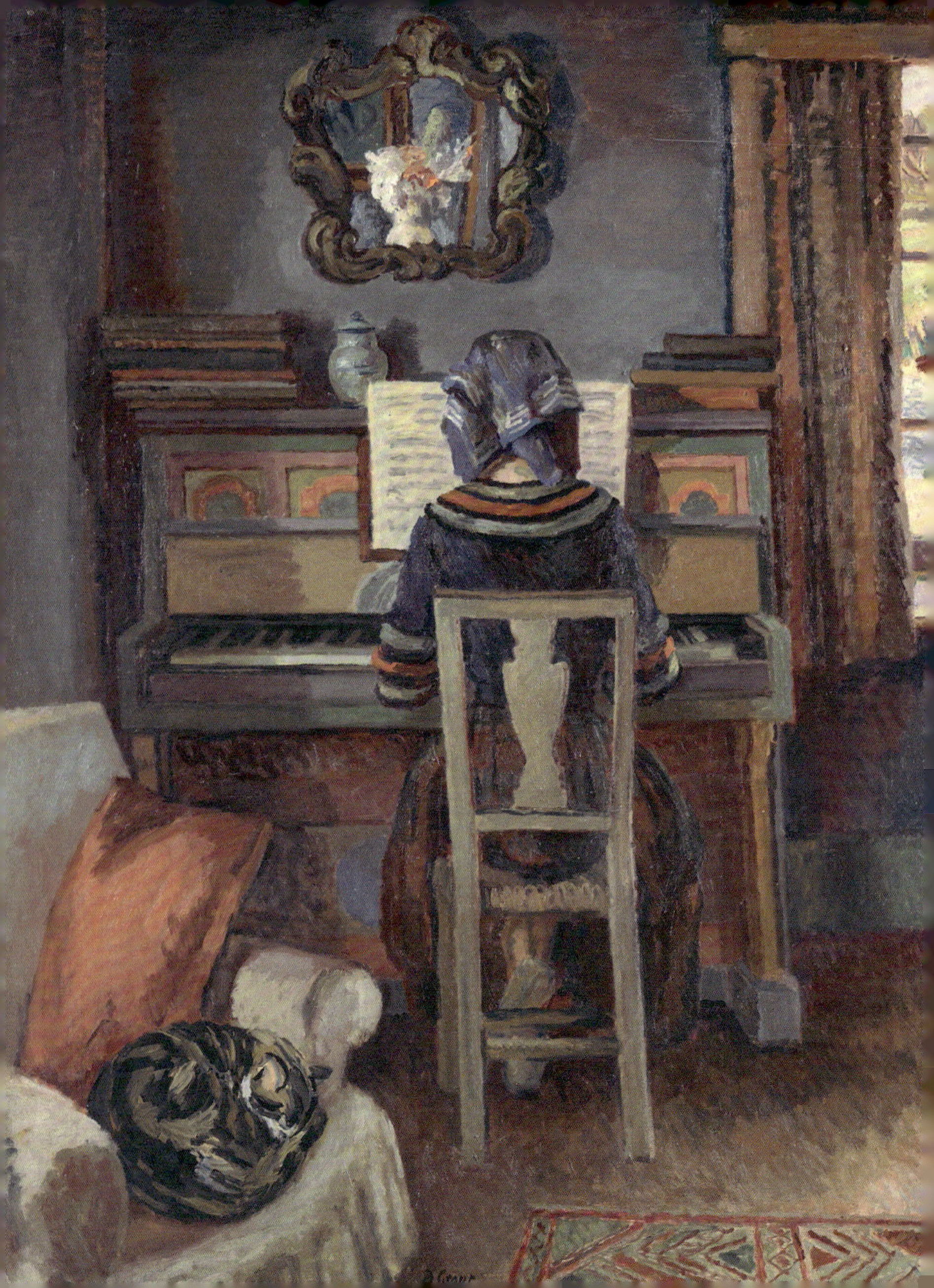

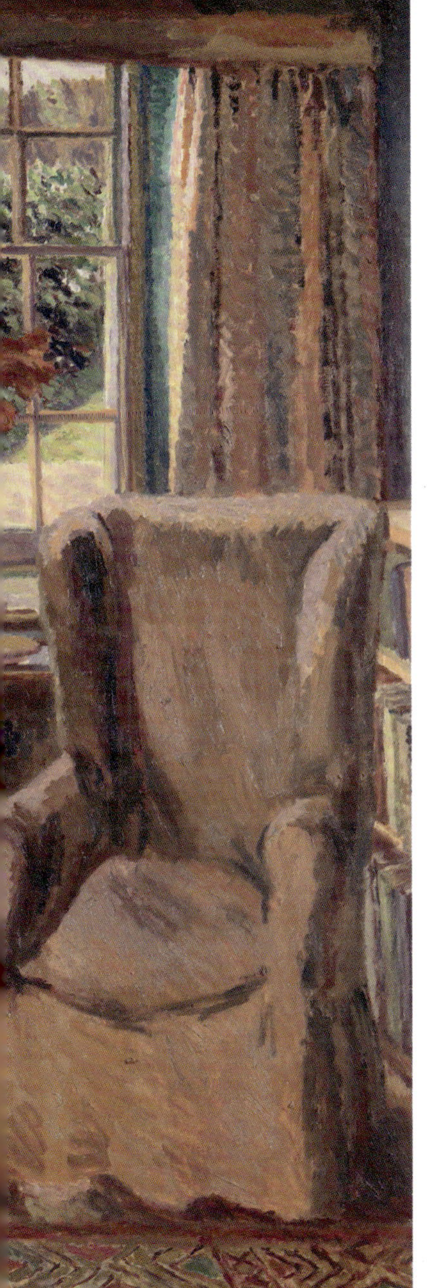

# The Cat's Meow

To the south of Zagazig in the eastern Nile Delta, quite unassuming in the suburban sprawl of the Egyptian city, lie the remains of an impressive structure: an elaborate labyrinth of crumbling walls, pillars and underground crypts that once made up the beautiful city of Bubastis (or Tell Basta). For centuries, hundreds of thousands of ancient Egyptians made pilgrimages to the city to visit the Temple of Bast, where they left mummified cats as offerings to the great cat goddess herself, Bastet.

Over 3,000 miles away in the sculpture gallery at the British Museum, London, a tourist is peering through a glass case to get a closer look at one of the institution's treasures; the Gayer-Anderson Cat, a 2,600-year-old bronze statue representing the same feline deity.

South of the river in London, Mildred the resident cat at Tate Modern is basking in the warm patch at the staff entrance, paying no heed to the security team locking up for the day.

Across the globe in Japan, Maneki-Neko cats wave silently and methodically from every shopfront, café, cat temple and bakery, and have been faithfully dispensing good fortune since the seventeenth century.

It is 1904 in Paris, and the Welsh artist Gwen John (1876–1939), is setting up her easel to capture the likeness of her dearly beloved, Edgar Quinet. This is not the first tribute she would devotedly paint of her tabby cat, nor the last.

Fast-forward over a hundred years, and a couple curled up on their sofa are deciding whether to watch *Black Panther* or the next episode of *Tiger King*. One checks their phone for an update on the news; Chief Mouser Larry is licking his paws outside number 10 Downing Street and getting a good angle for his paparazzi shot.

Night falls, as does the curtain in Seoul, South Korea. Another show done on the international tour of *Cats*, and Rum Tum Tugger is removing his whiskers until tomorrow, when he will paint them on again.

Out on the pavements, cats stalk the streets in the moonlight, while high above the Earth's atmosphere millions of images are transmitted via satellites so that Grumpy Cat and Lil Bub can be shared from Taiwan to Tennessee.

From deities to Dick Whittington, our feline friends have been immortalised in art and literature for thousands of years. The selection of artworks illustrated here showcase artists' endeavours over the past three centuries to capture the symbiotic relationship between cats and humans, uncovering images of companionship, domesticity and love, while acknowledging the contradictory history of the cat in Western visual art.

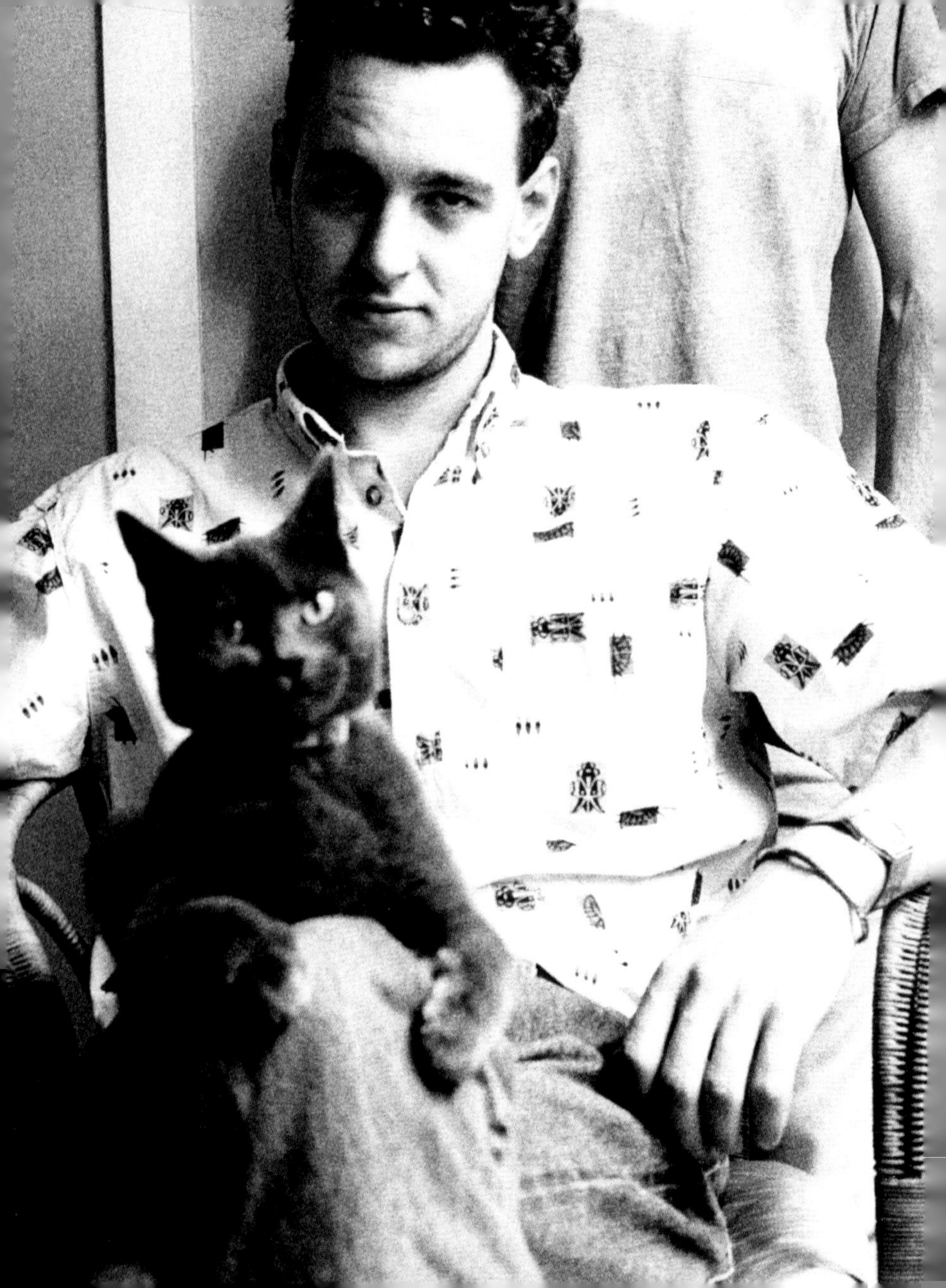

# Cats on Laps

Cats have been domesticated for around eight thousand years, but it was not until the eighteenth century that they began to appear in European art in their role as pets. Revered as gods in some countries, then chastised as agents of the Devil and witchcraft in others, cats have a chequered history across the globe, in both popular opinion and artistic symbolism, representing anything from trouble-making libertines to examples of licentious femininity. A cat on the lap in the following artworks can signify tranquillity and a sedentary life (pp.17 and 21) or it can hint at sexual frustrations (pp.11 and 13). The conflation of cats and female sexuality has a long tradition; from sex kittens to cat-hoarding spinsters, female sexuality has been something to be tamed or suspicious of. This chapter explores the diverse symbolism of cats sitting on laps. While some depictions have sexual connotations, many felines here are house cats and represent the epitome of domesticity, acting as companions and confidants to the human sitters whose laps have been miraculously graced by these felines.

**SUNIL GUPTA** *Roger & Steve, London* 1984, printed 2018 (detail, see p.18)

## RICHARD LINDNER

*Homage to a Cat* 1952

Using abstract eroticism, and inspired by the modernist painter Fernand Léger (1881–1955), German-born Lindner painted this monolithic woman and her cat while living in New York. He once claimed that live models disturbed him and he largely formed his works geometrically, which explains the awkward and imposing placements of his subjects on the canvas. The cat here certainly looks uncomfortable, and is trying to resist the strong arms of the woman who clutches it to her exposed breast. It could be said that this painting represents the power of female eroticism, as the cat struggles from a powerfully loving embrace.

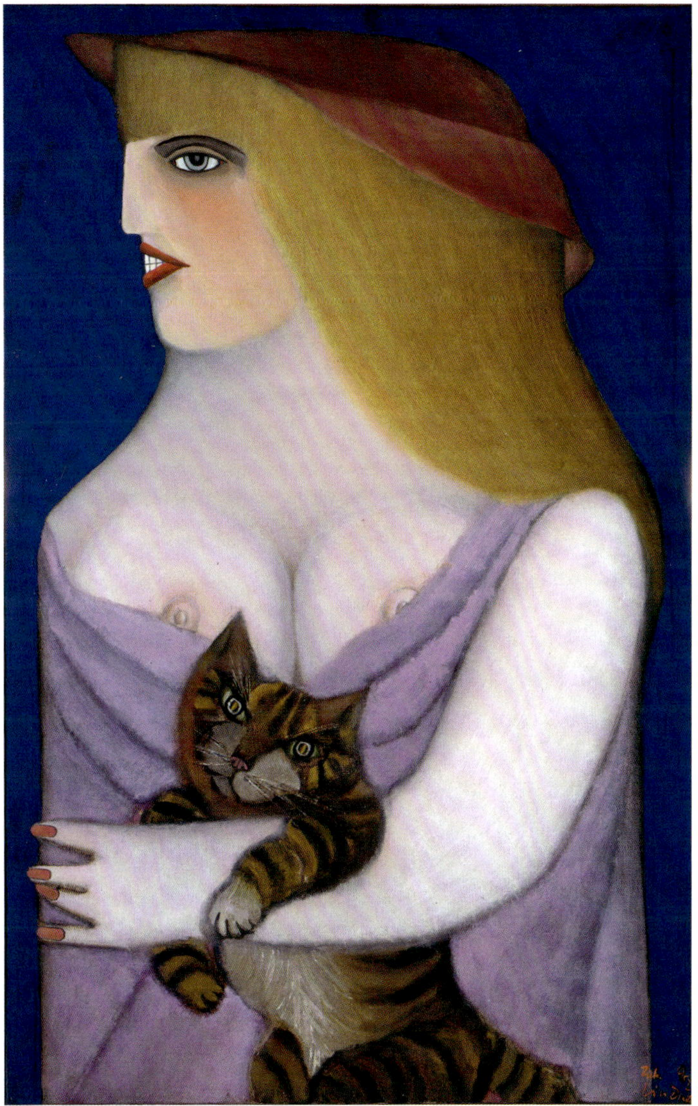

## DAVID HOCKNEY

***Mr and Mrs Clark and Percy*** 1970–1

Mr and Mrs Clark were friends of Hockney, and he was best man at their wedding. He claimed this painting was intended to capture the essence of their relationship. The white cat, Blanche (not Percy as the title suggests), on Ossie Clark's lap references the libertine – someone who has little regard for adhering to rules. The trope of including pets and animals to add meaning to human sitters is a well-known visual tool which also featured in *The Arnolfini Portrait* 1434 by Renaissance painter Jan van Eyck (1390–1441), where a tiny dog represents the couple's fidelity. Whether Hockney knew he was being prophetic with the inclusion of Blanche is unknown, but as fate would have it, the marriage sadly did not last.

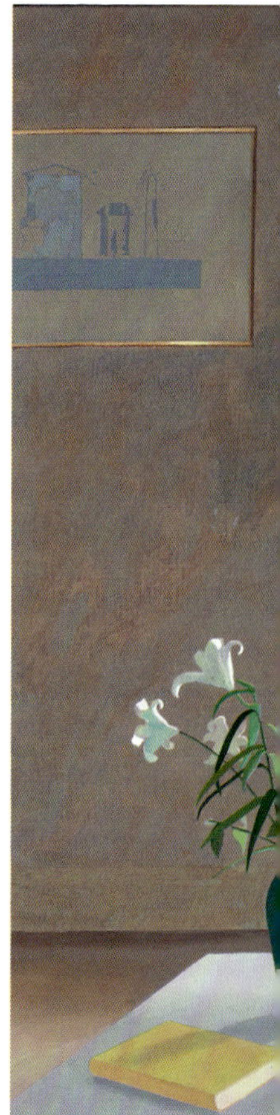

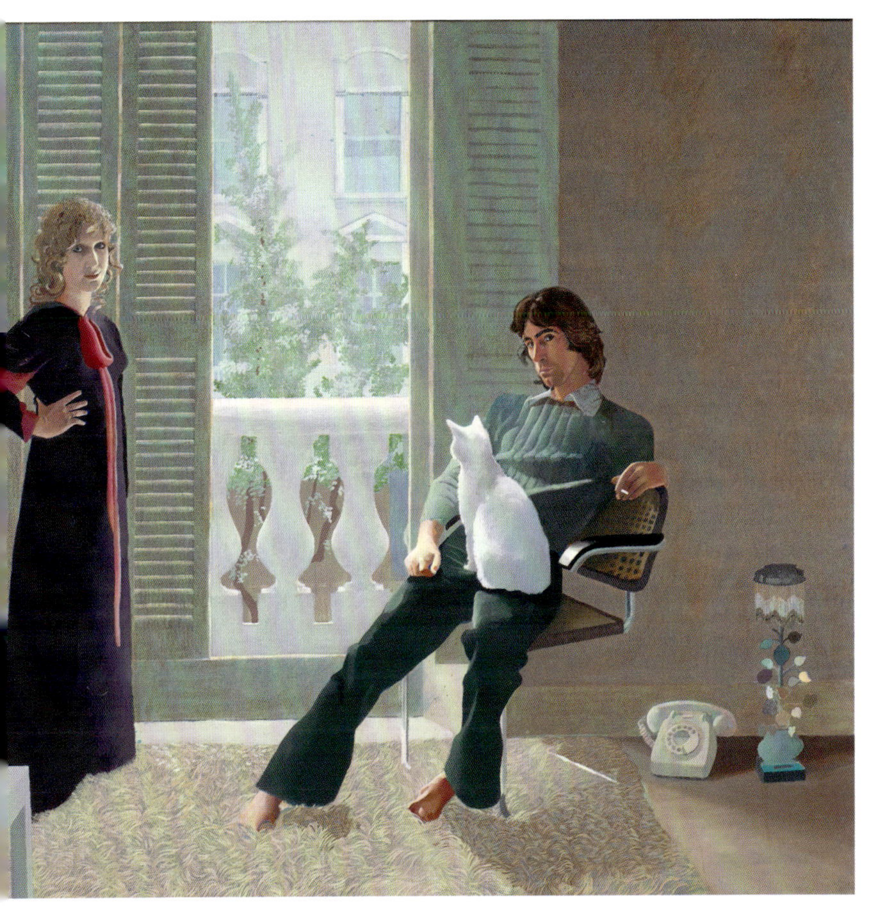

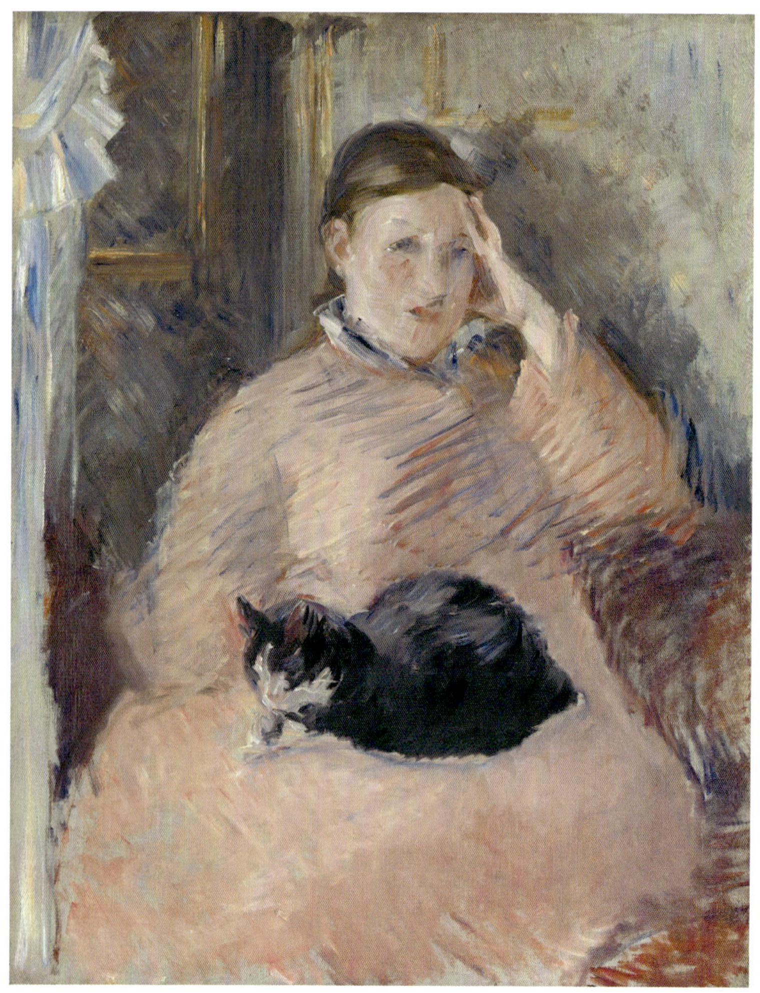

## EDOUARD MANET

*Woman with a Cat* c.1880

Manet was a French modernist painter and was dedicated to depicting life in the nineteenth century. Here his wife Suzanne sits comfortably in a domestic setting, with their cat Zizi resting on her lap. Manet was known to use cats as a metaphor for sexual temptation, but here we see a more sedate image of relaxed companionship and gentle familiarity as the pastel colours of Suzanne and Zizi blur into the walls around them. Manet painted this towards the end of his life, many years after the scandalous start of his lifelong relationship with Suzanne, who was once his family's piano teacher.

## J.M.W. TURNER

### *Cottage Interior by Firelight* 1790–1

The hazy blue mountains, golden sunsets and stormy seas that we are all so familiar with in the works of English romantic artist, J.M.W. Turner, are here turned inside out. We find ourselves not gazing out across a watercolour vista, but inwards to an open fire in a rustic interior. Flames lick up the chimney, casting long shadows from the figures gathered around it, while the moon can be seen in the night sky through the window. It is an idealised scene of pastoral kindness, with the figure on the floor offering a spoonful of dinner to the cat. Despite the clear lack of means for this charming group, no one shall go hungry tonight.

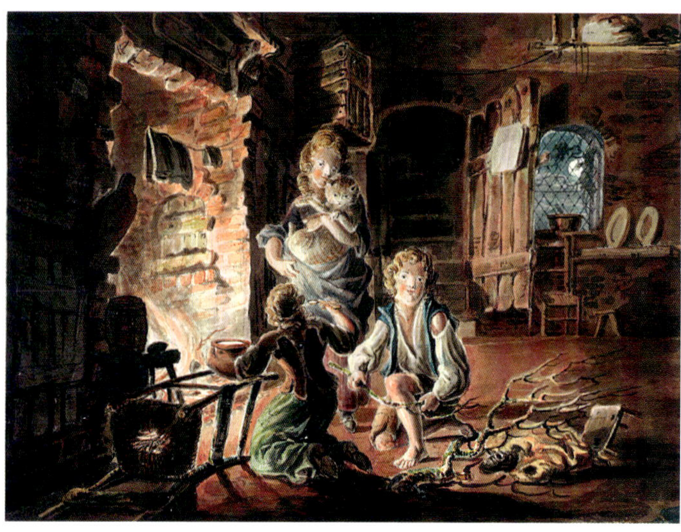

## JOHN NASH

*Window Plants* 1945

An elderly lady and her cat sleep contentedly in their home, botanicals on the windowsill blending two worlds – the domestic and the wild. Zebra cactus, and other popular houseplants, prominently line the foreground of the painting, while details create a floral frame around the canvas. Nash was commissioned to make this work as part of the School Prints scheme, where well-known artists created lithographs which could be pinned to classroom walls. This image would have shown a familiar world to children, encouraging them to see art all around them, where anyone, even a granny and her cat, can be models.

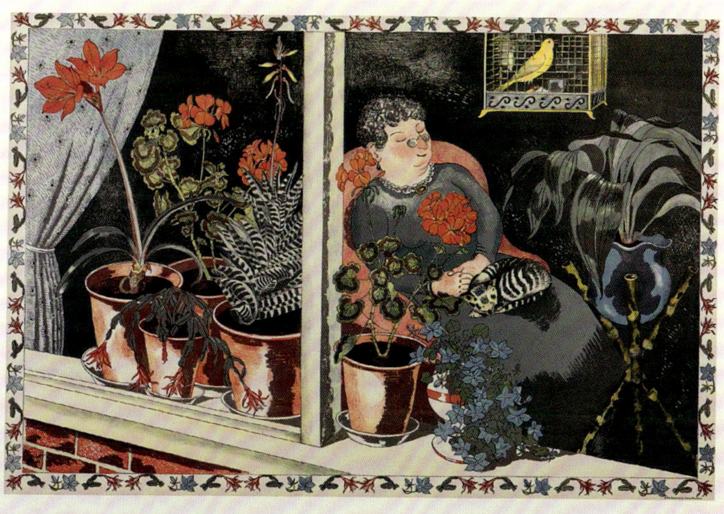

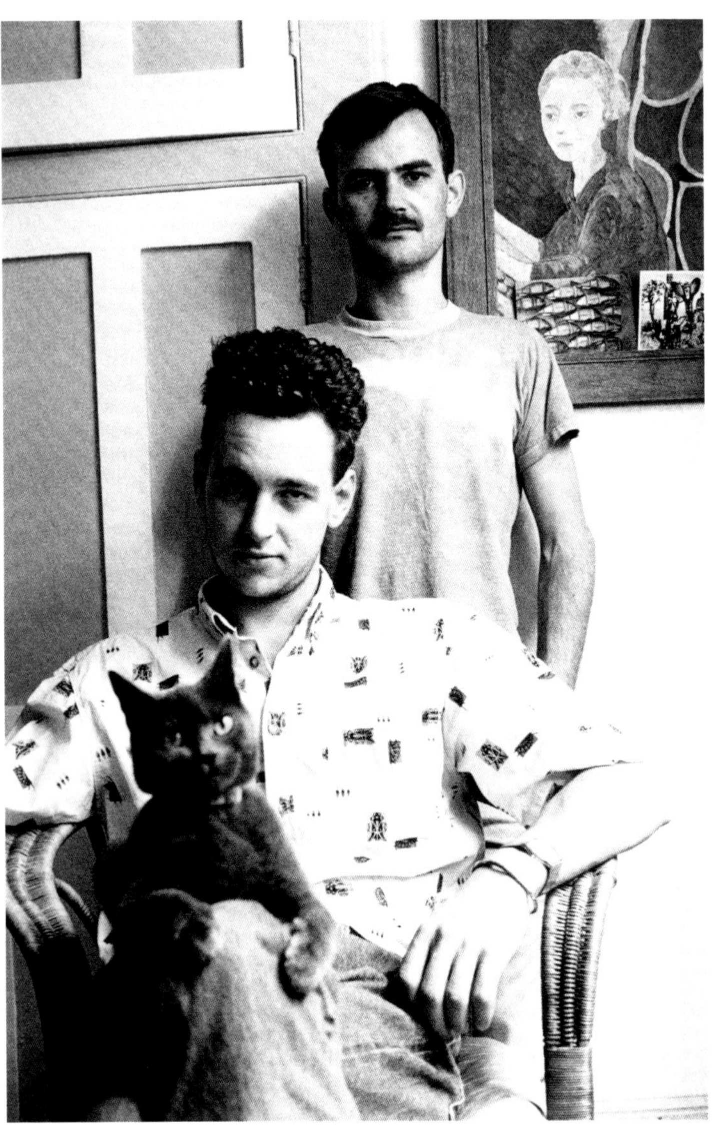

## SUNIL GUPTA

***Roger & Steve, London*** 1984, printed 2018

This is one of a group of over thirty photographs taken from Gupta's *Lovers: Ten Years On*, a series of black-and-white portraits of gay couples taken in the UK between 1984 and 1986. The couple here pose with their cat, which views the camera lens with a questioning intensity. Gupta accompanied the series with an artist's statement about gay self-consciousness and the turning of public opinion against the acceptance of homosexuality. During the AIDS crisis representations of gay people were predominantly stereotyped as deviant, sometimes dangerous. The inclusion of the cat in this portrait directly challenges those homophobic assumptions, paralleling the traditional portraits of family units with a domestic stability.

## ETHEL WALKER

*The Hon. Mrs Adams* c.1901

Walker was a Scottish painter known for her still-life flowers, sapphic seascapes and her colourful impressionistic portraits, typically of talented and beautiful young women. Here the colours are muted but the expression of her sitter most certainly is not. The Honourable Mrs Adams is animated and convivial; her feline companion dozing carefree upon her lap, the whites of its whiskers caught in Walker's free brushwork.

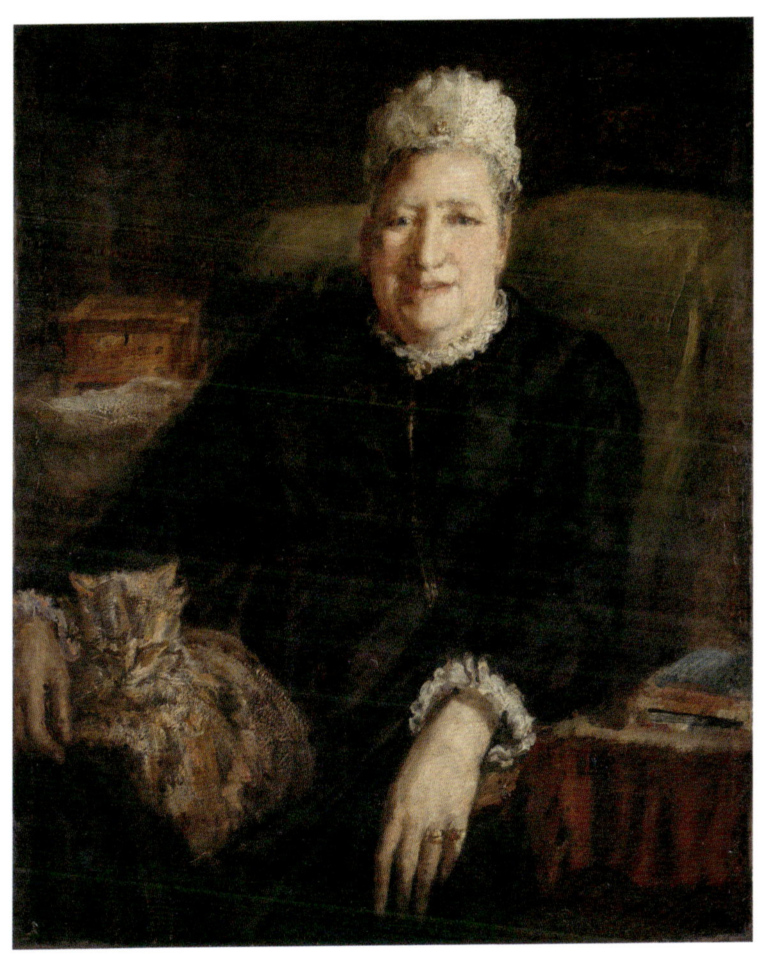

## GWEN JOHN

*Young Woman Holding a Black Cat* c.1920–5

Black cats are now synonymous with witchcraft, after years of superstition and folklore claiming the animals as witches' familiars or omens of bad luck. Gwen John, endlessly unlucky in her own love affairs, kept a great many cats, and conforms to the 'mad cat lady' trope, living in solitude and feeding her adored felines expensive pâté. John used this enigmatic sitter as the subject for numerous portraits, although the young model remains unknown. The cat has nonchalantly turned its back on us.

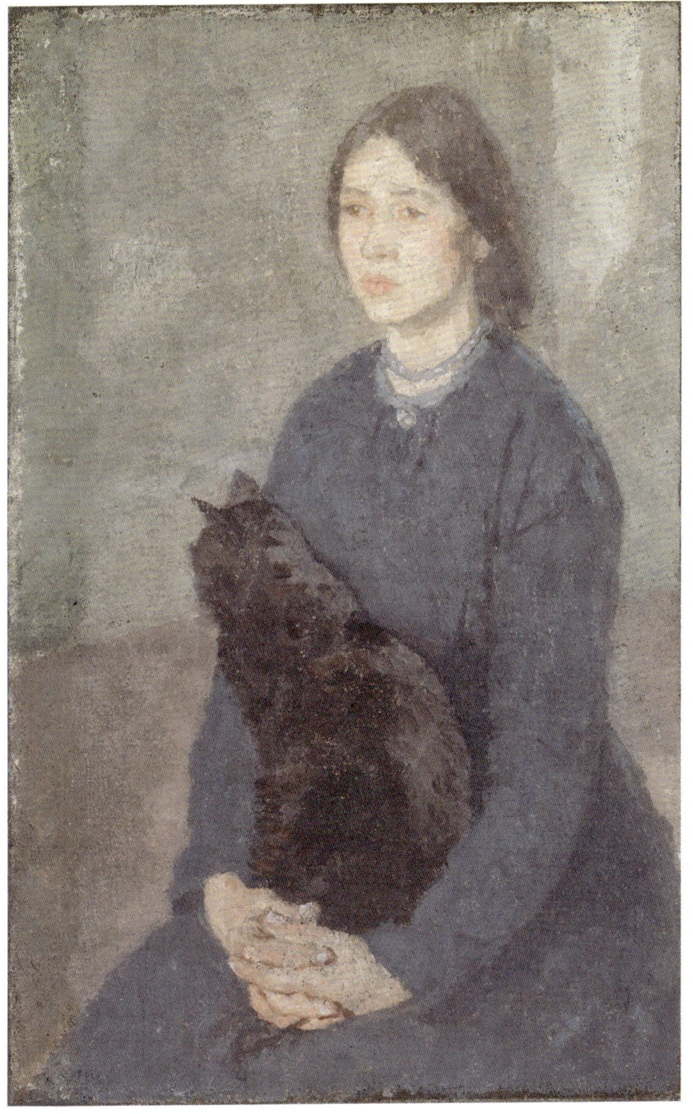

## NIGEL HENDERSON

***Photograph of an unidentified girl holding a Siamese cat***
c.1949–56

Siamese cats are known to be affectionate and highly intelligent. The attention of this one appears to be elsewhere, and although the black-and-white image cheats us of colour, we know those big eyes are a perfect azure blue, particular to the breed. Perhaps those Pantone peepers are fixed on a bird outside the window or a leaf blowing in the wind. The girl, however, only has eyes for the cat on her lap; she has succumbed to the power of a beautiful feline and is totally and utterly besotted.

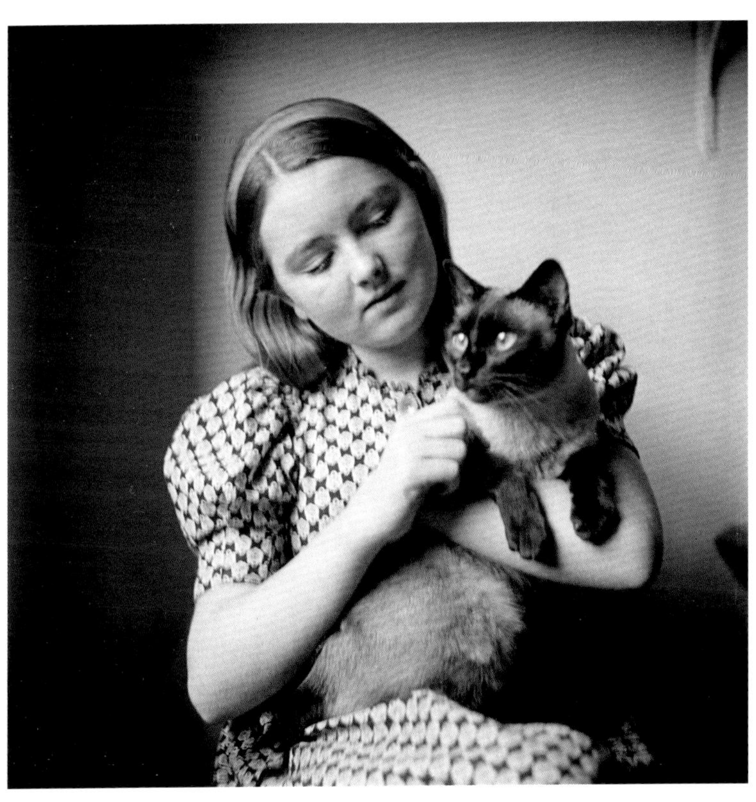

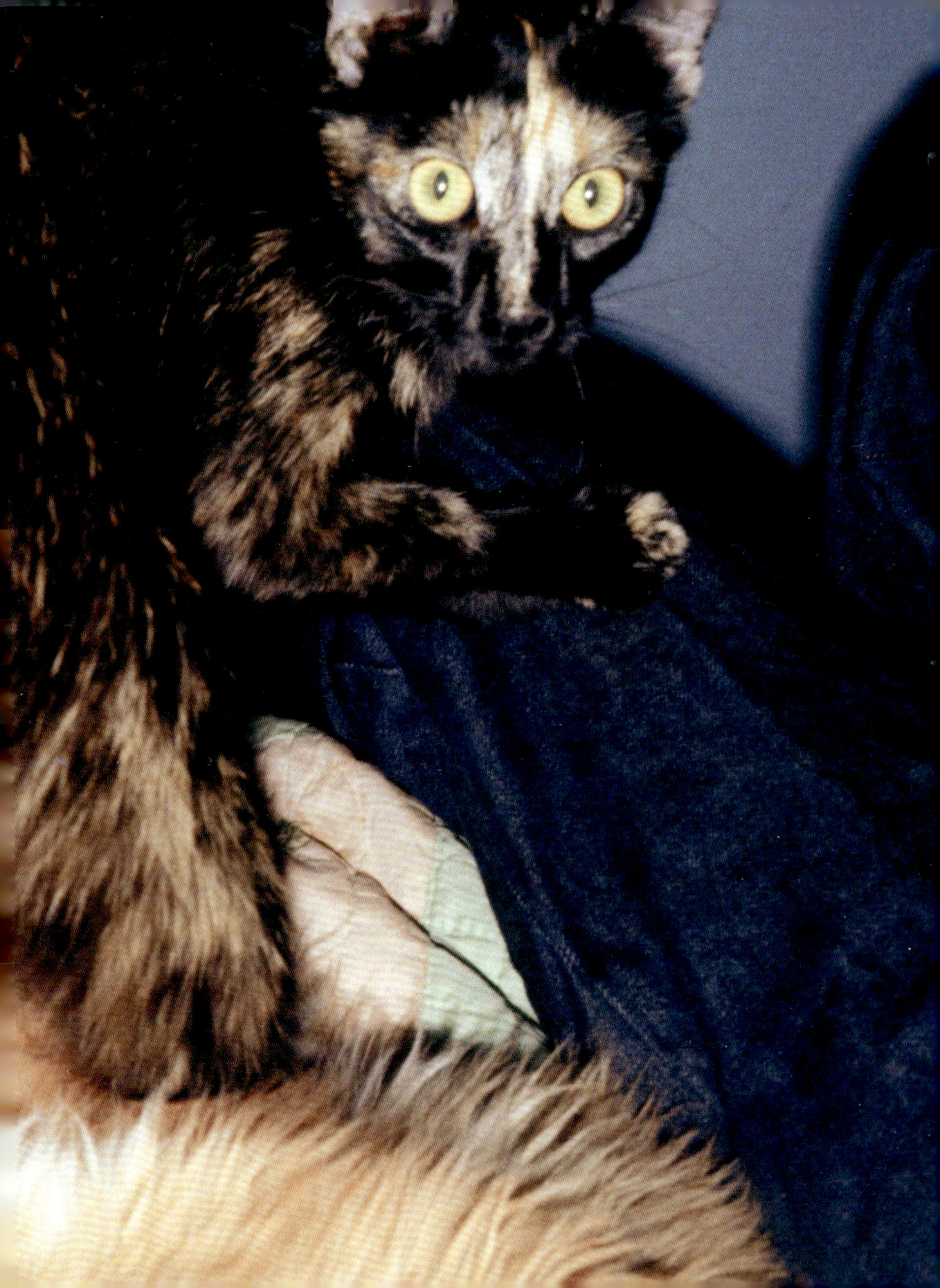

# Snap Cat

Photographs of cats are some of the most viewed images on the Internet. Any explorers of Internet search engines or social media will have at some point stumbled across a cat meme or 'lolcat'. This form of rapidly evolving Internet art morphs as quickly as a TikTok star can hit one million views with a single video. Chances are, if you are looking at a viral photograph of a cat then it has been through several iterations already, has been shared around the world and probably has its own franchise. But why are we so obsessed with photographs of cats? Perhaps it is because we are natural voyeurs and we enjoy seeing candid snapshots of cats' private lives. Some suggest that looking at photographs of cats releases endorphins in the same way that petting them does – maybe that is why we are hooked on taking and searching for photographs of them. Or is it because a photograph of a cat captures an unguarded moment? The cat is always unapologetic for what it is doing, whether banal or discerning. Whatever the reason, we are compelled to look at them, and these artists probably were, too.

**STEPHEN SHORE** *Canyon, Texas, July 1972* 1972, printed 2006 (detail, see p.31)

## PRUNELLA CLOUGH

*Black and white photograph of a cat winding itself around a man's legs* 1950s

Clough was a printmaker and painter who, while studying art, became a draughtsman for an engineer during the Second World War. This experience may well have been the inspiration for her early works, which are characterised by urban and working landscapes. Her photographs usually act as a reference library from which she could later work. However this image appears to be an anomaly, as it does not seem to have been used for any other purpose. Written on the back of the photograph is 'DC Lancashire', which might identify the legs belonging to her friend and fellow artist, David Carr. The cat, however, remains unknown.

*Colour photograph of a cat in a window* 1986

Almost all of Clough's photographs in the Tate collection are of industrial landscapes: cranes, cooling and gas towers, and coal mines. The images here are unusual in featuring cats, a startlingly soft diversion among the harshness of her usual scenes. Clough's photographs provided snapshots she could return to, to use as studies or moods for her paintings. Usually landscapes are reduced to core textures: fissures in rocks, foam on waves, lichen on flint walls, crumples in tarpaulin. Here textures are domestic; the gauze of a net curtain, a whisker pressed against glass.

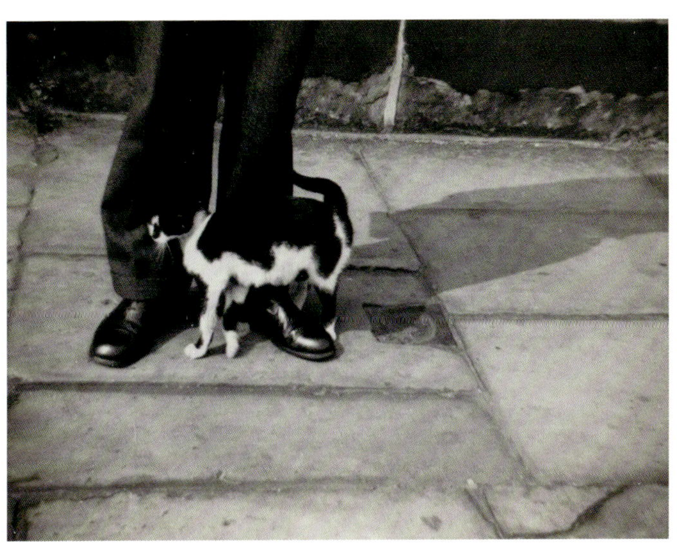

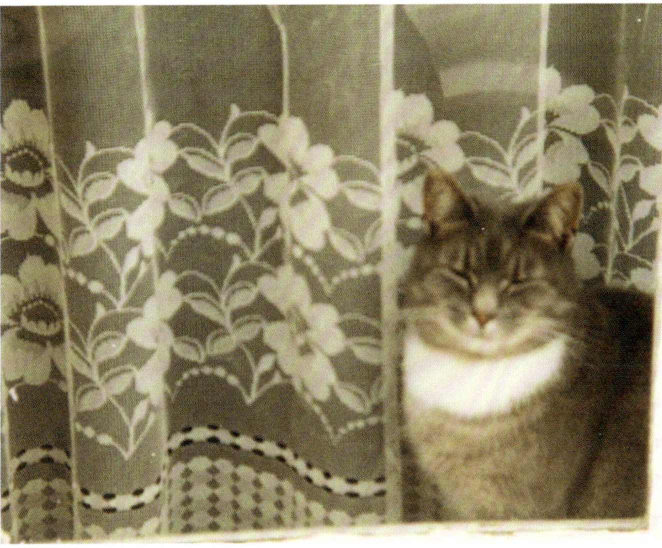

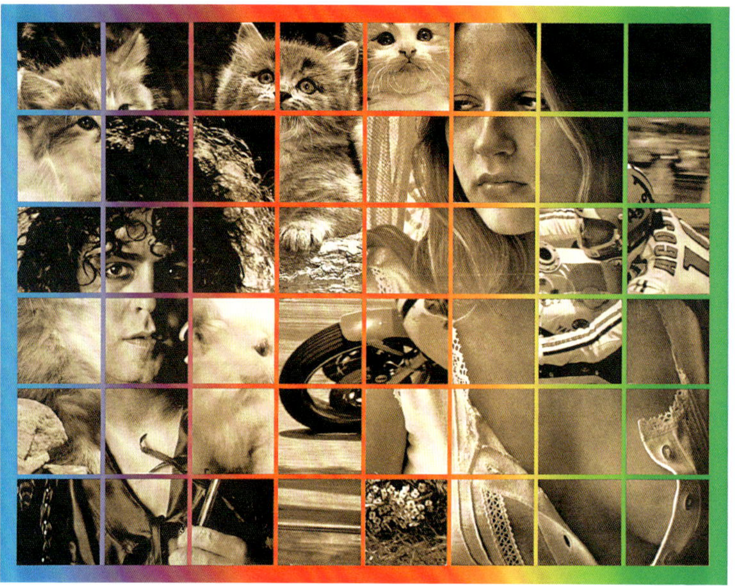

## PETER PHILLIPS

*Six Times Eight, Dreaming* 1974

Sex and drugs and rock 'n' roll (and cats). The kittens here provide pop artist Phillips with a timeless and well-used metaphor for coitus, while rockstar Marc Bolan (1947–77) brings the 1970s glam and Grand-Prix racer Giacomo Agostini (b.1942) the adrenalin. Smoking wheels and sultry gazes make for some real cool cats, but the unknown entity is the woman, whose pose and state of undress is a typical example of commercialising bohemian sexual liberation.

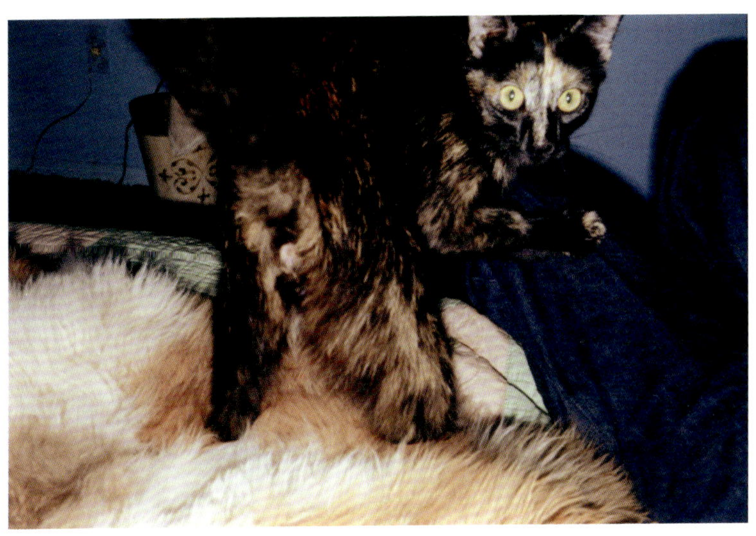

## STEPHEN SHORE

***Canyon, Texas, July 1972*** 1972, printed 2006

This cat is behaving as most cats do. The sofa on which it stands is its territory, and the leg on which one paw possessively rests, is also hers. Unblinking and unabashed, this cat has been caught in a compromising snapshot, the aesthetic of which was badly received by photography critics at the time for being too radical. Since then this particular series from Shore has been acknowledged as a significant moment in the history of photography, as digital colour photography starts to claim its space in the canon.

## EILEEN AGAR

***Photograph of Bella the cat lying down*** c.1936

This photograph is perhaps titled incorrectly, as Bella, Eileen Agar's cat (potentially a Turkish Angora shorthair), appears to be in a pose of slight agitation rather than lying down. Cast in full sunlight, it is likely that just moments before, Bella had been basking in the warm patch on the floor of Agar's studio in West London before being rudely disturbed. This cat is part of Agar's photographic archive, which documents her trips around the UK and abroad.

## FELICITAS VOGLER

***Photograph of Ben Nicholson holding his cat, Tommy*** 1968

Vogler was an impressive landscape photographer, outstandingly knowledgeable on all things from philosophy to binomial nomenclature (the naming of plants and trees), and worked as a semi-professional astrologist throughout her life. Such broad interests made her an avid conversationalist, which is likely how she and her husband Ben Nicholson established a rapport, before marrying two months after meeting. Vogler was very particular; she disliked noise and art historians, but she liked cats and Beethoven. Here Tommy, their cat, throws a paw carelessly over Nicholson's shoulder, while Nicholson himself engages with the camera, proudly showing off his cherished pet.

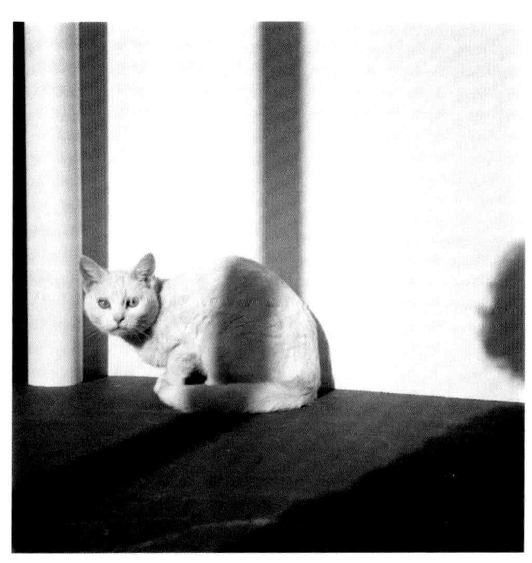

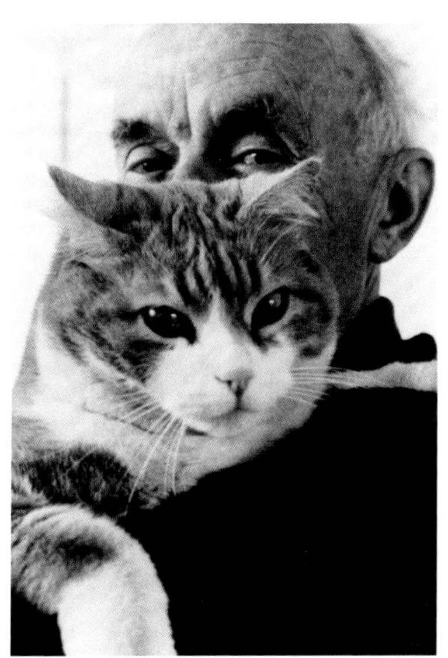

## BRUCE DAVIDSON

*Girl holding kitten* 1960

American photographer Bruce Davidson was known for photographing those on the fringes of society, from gangs in Brooklyn to travelling circus performers. Referring to himself as an 'outsider on the inside', he was given unprecedented access to communities that were traditionally hostile to outsiders. The girl in this photo is unknown, even to Davidson, and he claimed it was pure chance he met her after she took him into an underground dancehall. Sleeping mat slung over the shoulder, a tiny kitten in her hands and an open face, she epitomises the lost urban cat; a shadow in the street.

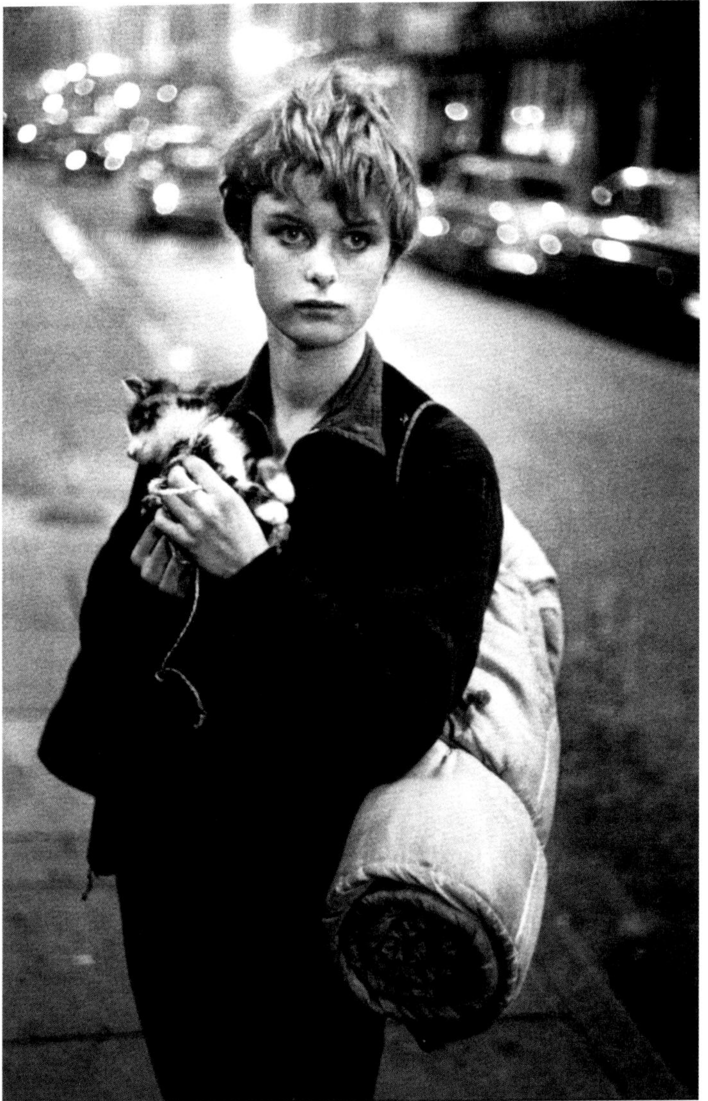

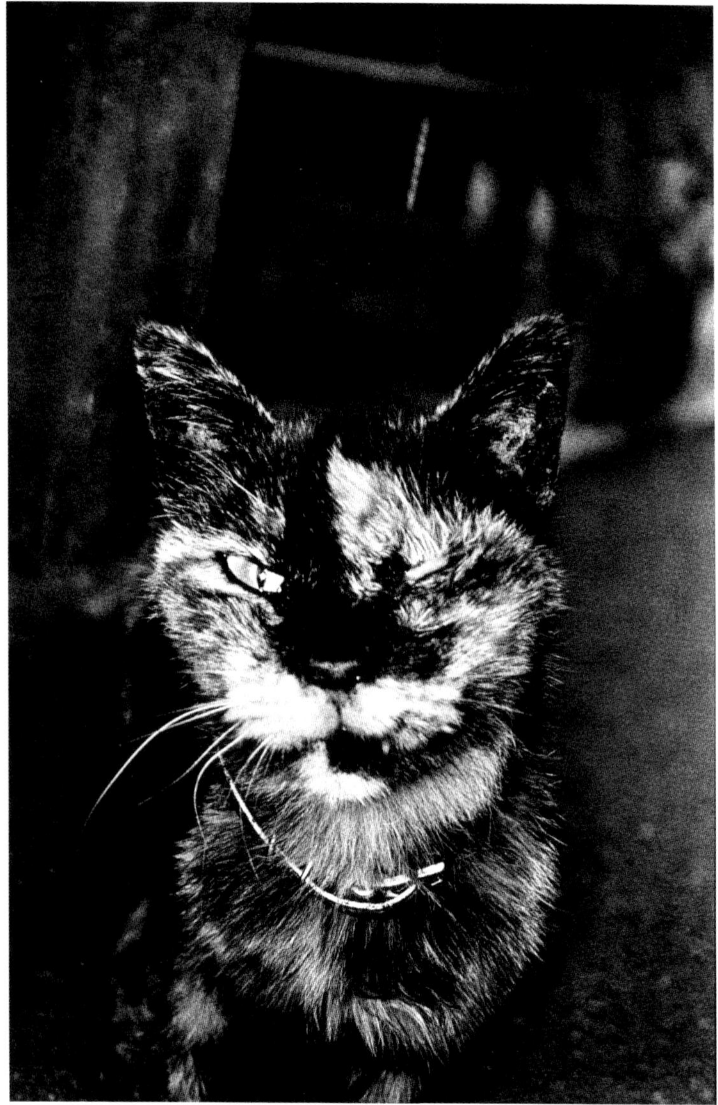

## DAIDO MORIYAMA

***Memory*** 2012

One milky eye half jammed shut, the other intently glaring into the camera lens, this feline is not one you would want to meet down a dark alley. Moriyama's work embraces the Japanese aesthetic of wabi-sabi, or finding beauty in imperfection, which is perhaps why he was drawn to this cat. There is just one small indication that this ragtag moggy is not like every other rough street cat who has seen better days: the collar round its neck shows us that perhaps this cat has a home and that someone, somewhere adores this puss despite its somewhat bristly appearance.

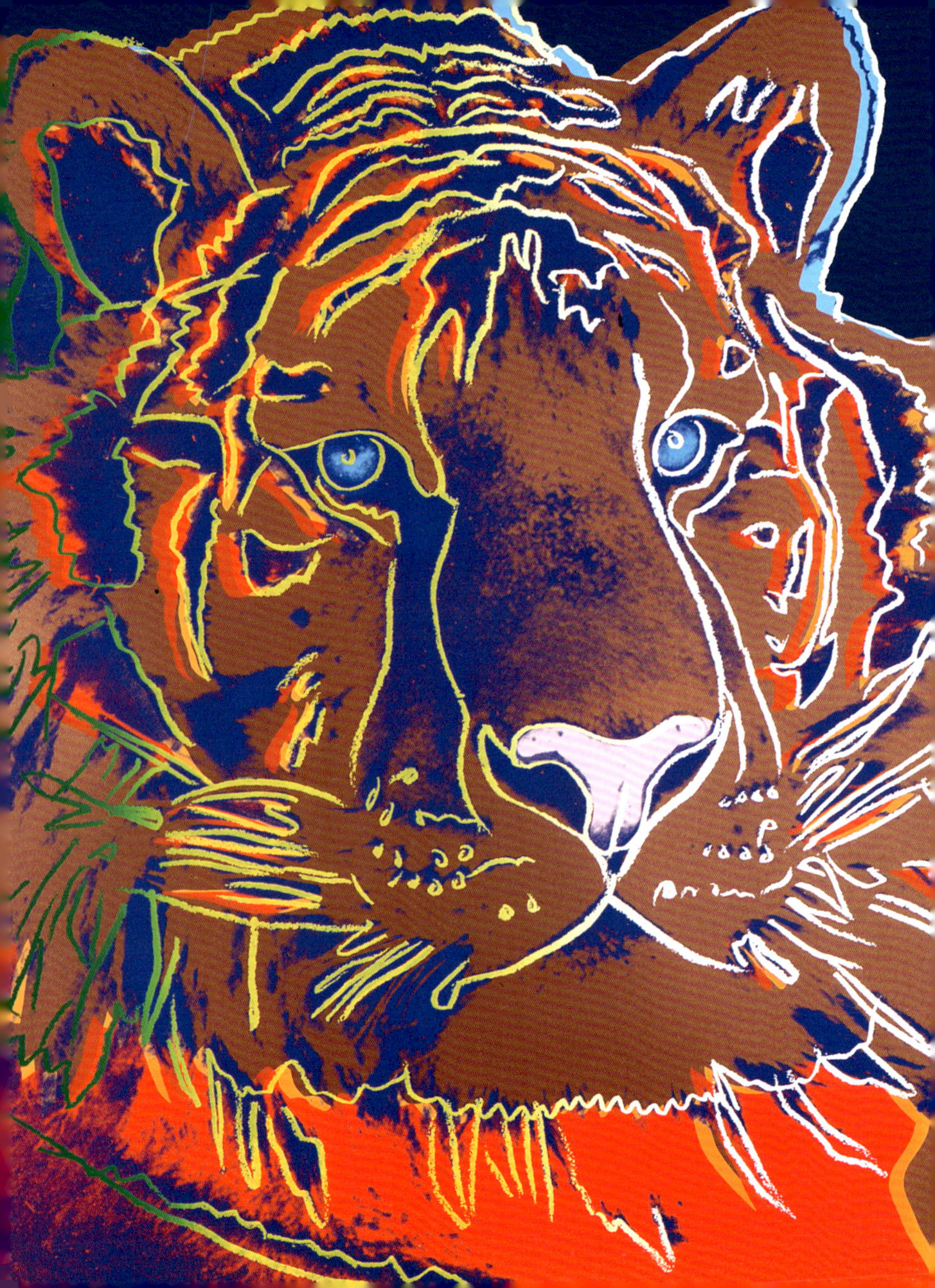

# Fierce Cats

With over thirty-eight species of cat in the world, it is some of the biggest that have inspired artists. With an illustrious history in visual culture across Africa, Asia and Europe, the lion has enjoyed a status like no other animal in the world and maintains its position of king of the beasts to this day. Universal symbols of power, nobility and bravery, lions were first recorded on the walls of caves in France some 32,000 years ago, and their enduring prowess has led them on a colourful journey as guardians to temples, gateways to cities; through illuminated manuscripts and as heraldic emblems for royalty; as messianic beasts in magical worlds accessed through wardrobes, and as blockbuster animations in the form of Simba and Nala. Other wild cats, such as the tiger, are held in similarly high esteem and are revered across the globe from China to Oklahoma. The biggest of all cats, the tiger maintains an impression of 'exoticism' in Western art. Lone animals, tigers present somewhat as solitary enigmas, stalking and mysterious (p.51) but with a potent power that has been used by artists such as Chila Kumari Singh Burman, to signify radical feminism and its association with Hindu warrior goddess, Durga.

**ANDY WARHOL** *Siberian Tiger* 1983
(detail, see p.41)

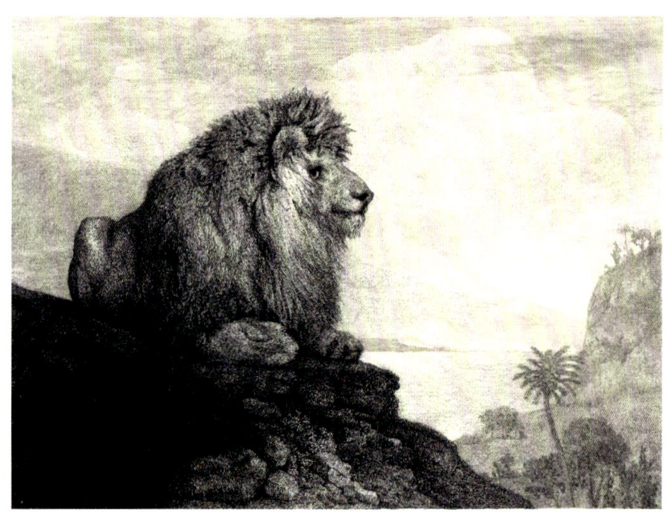

**GEORGE STUBBS**

***A Lion Resting on a Rock*** published 1788

A fearsome creature sits upon the prow of a rock. The mighty, powerful king surveys his territory, terrible to behold and awesome in his magnificent power ... or maybe not quite. This lion has a rather simpering look, and his giant teddy-bear paws are comfortably folded beneath him much like a house cat. The detailed lines of the engraving give the impression of a great mound of fluff for a mane. An understandably modified depiction when one realises that Stubbs imagined this setting and drew from memory the tamed Barbary lions he saw in the menagerie at the Tower of London.

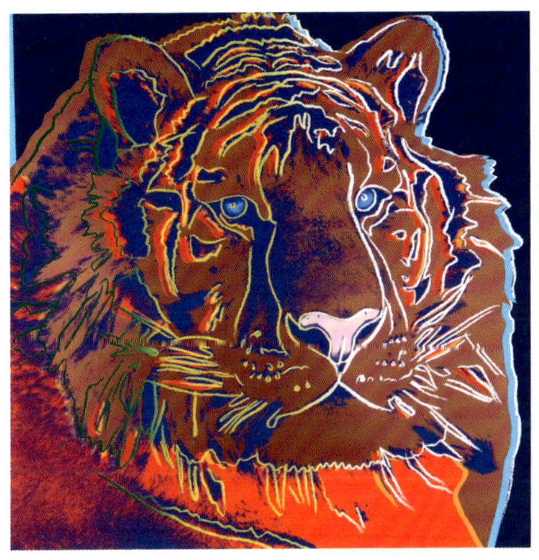

**ANDY WARHOL**

***Siberian Tiger*** 1983

Warhol was a true eccentric cat lover, having made an artist book (ungrammatically) titled *25 Cats Name Sam and One Blue Pussy* (1987), which was literally just that. It is perhaps less widely known that he also had a keen interest in ecological issues and animal welfare, and was commissioned by environmentalist art collectors, Ronald and Frayda Feldman to bring these animals into public consciousness and give them the star treatment. *Endangered Species* 1983, is a set of ten screenprints highlighting animals around the world on the extinction list. Almost forty years after the making of these 'animals in makeup', the Siberian Tiger sadly remains on that list.

## UNKNOWN ARTIST

***Black and white photograph of Ian Breakwell's 'Circus' a photo-silkscreen collage featuring the heads of a cat, lion, tiger, warthog and giraffe above a circus ring*** 1978

In January 2020 it became illegal in the UK for travelling circuses to perform with wild animals, but Ian Breakwell's circus project is not a record of a bygone era when wild cats would be used as bait to bring in the punters. His circus 'is a custard pie in the eye of that normal, rational, repressive world in which everything has its proper place'. The posters he made are for a fabricated circus act; a satirical illusion of the hierarchies in society in which the ringmasters and cats are performing one monumental act. This photo-silkscreen makes up just one part of Breakwell's exhibition, *Circus*.

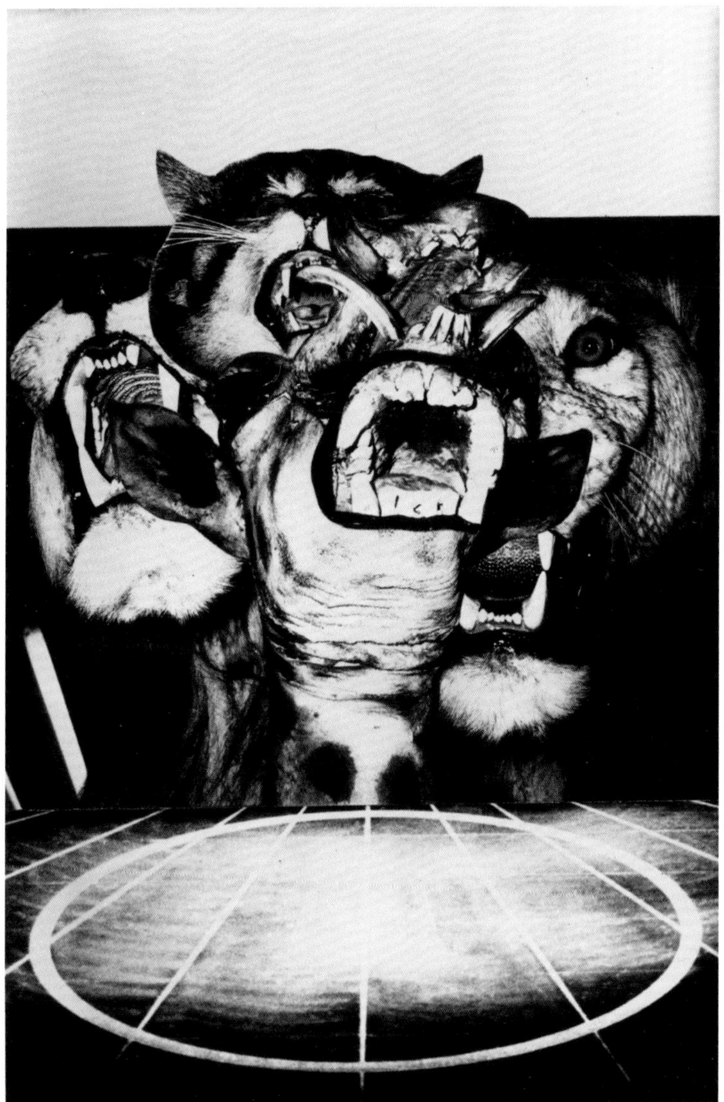

## KARL WESCHKE

*Tiger Tiger* 1953

Weschke was born in Germany and came to the UK as a prisoner of war. After his release he studied art, but found himself struggling to make ends meet and became the assistant to a lion-feeder at a London circus. It was here that he made drawings and prints of circus animals, including many versions of this tiger woodcut, which is heavily influenced by German expressionism. He inked the block with different colours for every print, so each is unique. Later he moved to Cornwall and joined the Penwith Society of Arts, painting the surrounding landscapes and his dog.

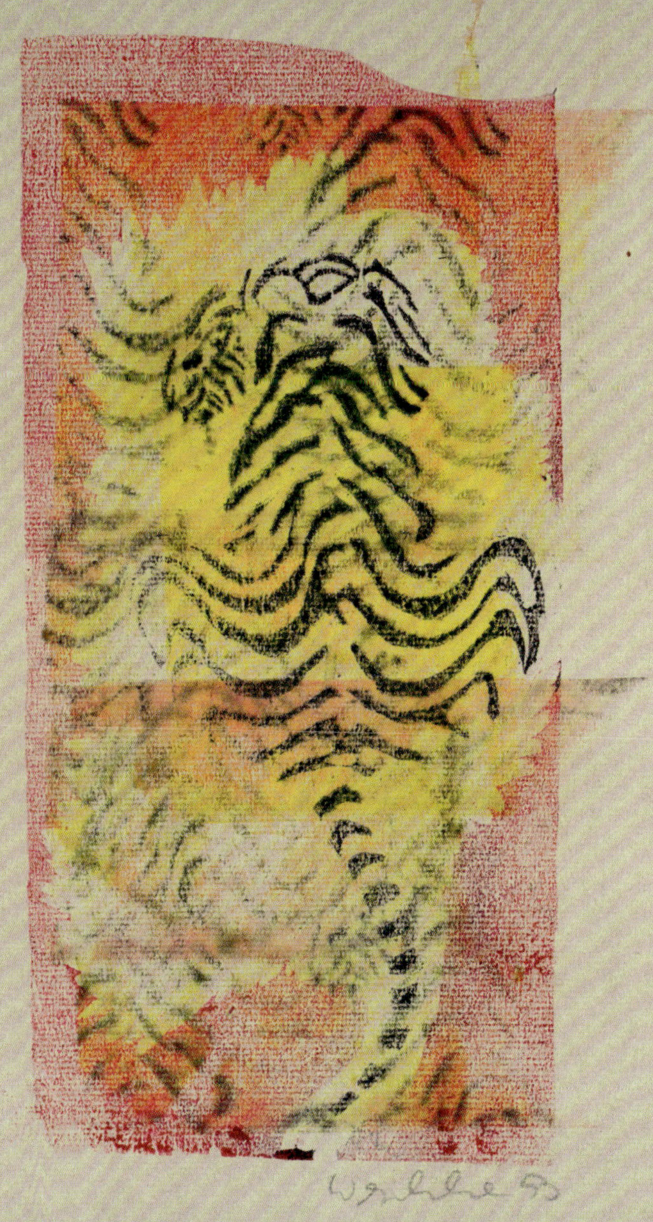

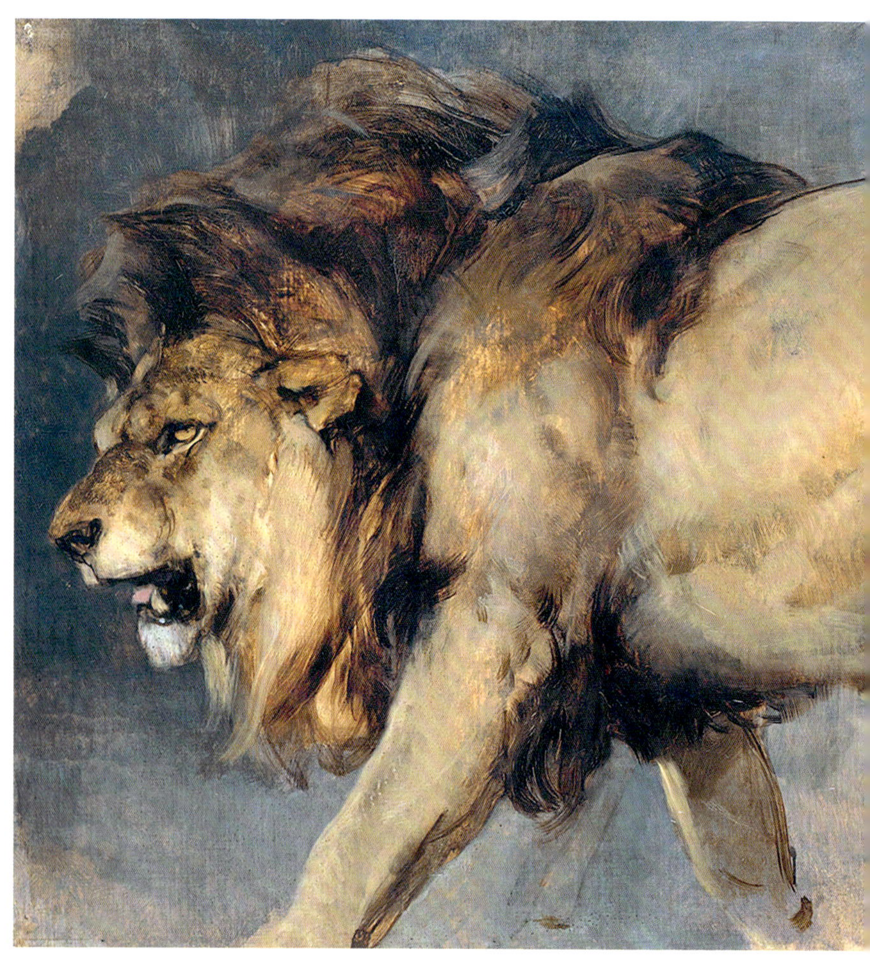

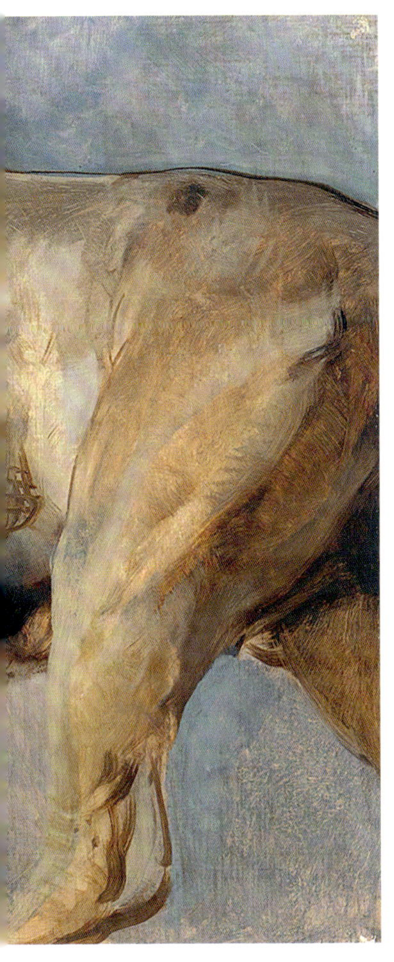

## EDWIN HENRY LANDSEER

***Study of a Lion*** c.1862

This study was likely used for Landseer's most famous big cats: the iconic lions at the base of Nelson's Column in Trafalgar Square, London. In fact, John Ballantyne's portrait of Landseer shows this study propped up in his studio, alongside a lion skin and hair for reference. Landseer was undoubtedly a dog person rather than a cat lover. The lions took him almost a decade to complete and their creation, alongside substance abuse, is said to have contributed to a breakdown in his health. In Ballantyne's painting, Landseer's faithful dog, Lassie, rests between the great paws, unaffected by the giant felines around him.

## JOHN FREDERICK LEWIS

***Head of a Lion*** 1824

With a carefully coiffed quiff and plaintive expression, this big cat bears a resemblance to the Cowardly Lion from the 1939 production of *The Wizard of Oz*. Lewis, an English Orientalist, although known now for his detailed depictions of Middle-Eastern interiors, started his career as an animal painter and trained with the great Edwin Landseer, producing a series of big cat prints, in which most are shown dozing off.

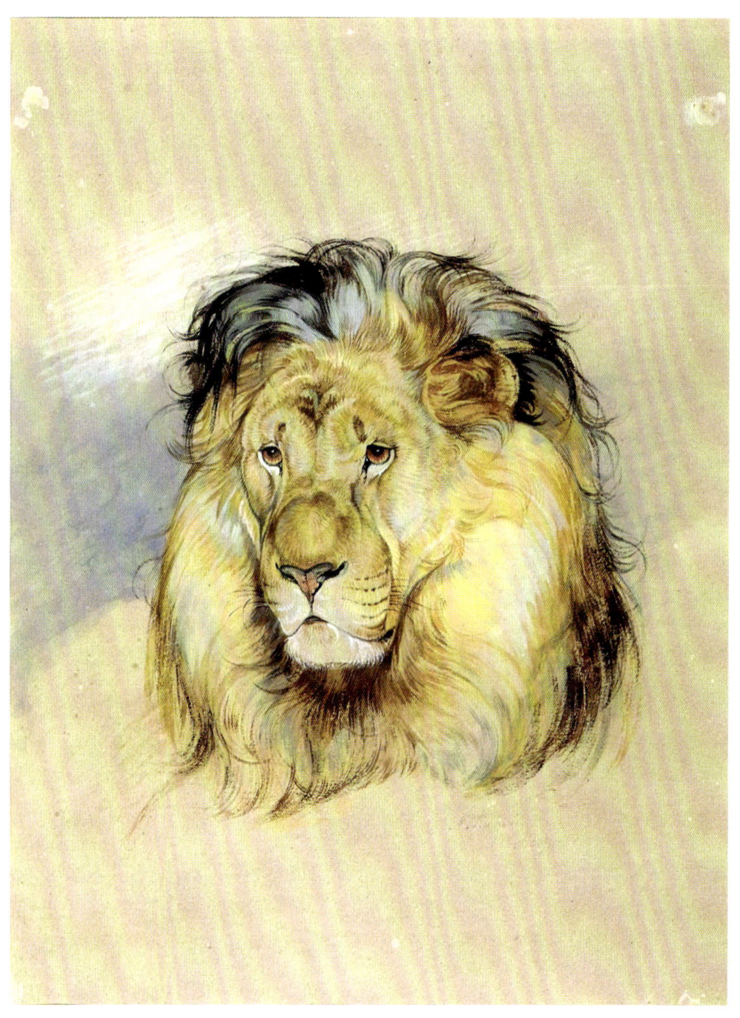

## MISCH KOHN

*Tiger* 1949

Kohn was an iconic American printmaker who started his career in the wake of the Great Depression – a time especially difficult for artists, whose work was deemed dispensable. After spending a year in Mexico he began his first larger-scale engravings, including his most famed, *Tiger*, inspired by William Blake's poem (*The Tyger*). The print itself carries specific visual references in its angular shapes – 'thy fearful symmetry' – but Kohn described the print in terms of form rather than context – 'everything about it was divided up into planes ... with certain qualities or organisation of the space, so that the movement would be abstract, carried through the landscape'.

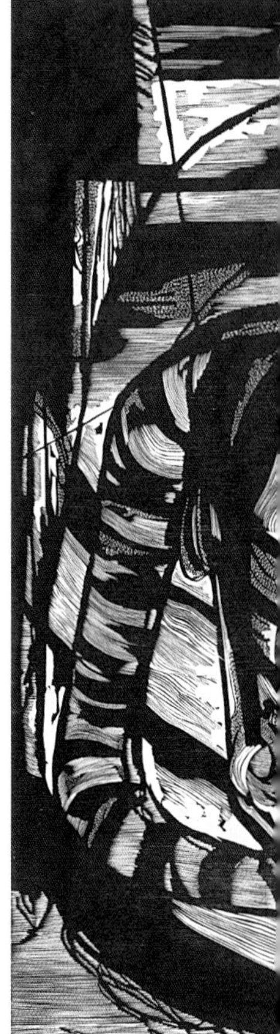

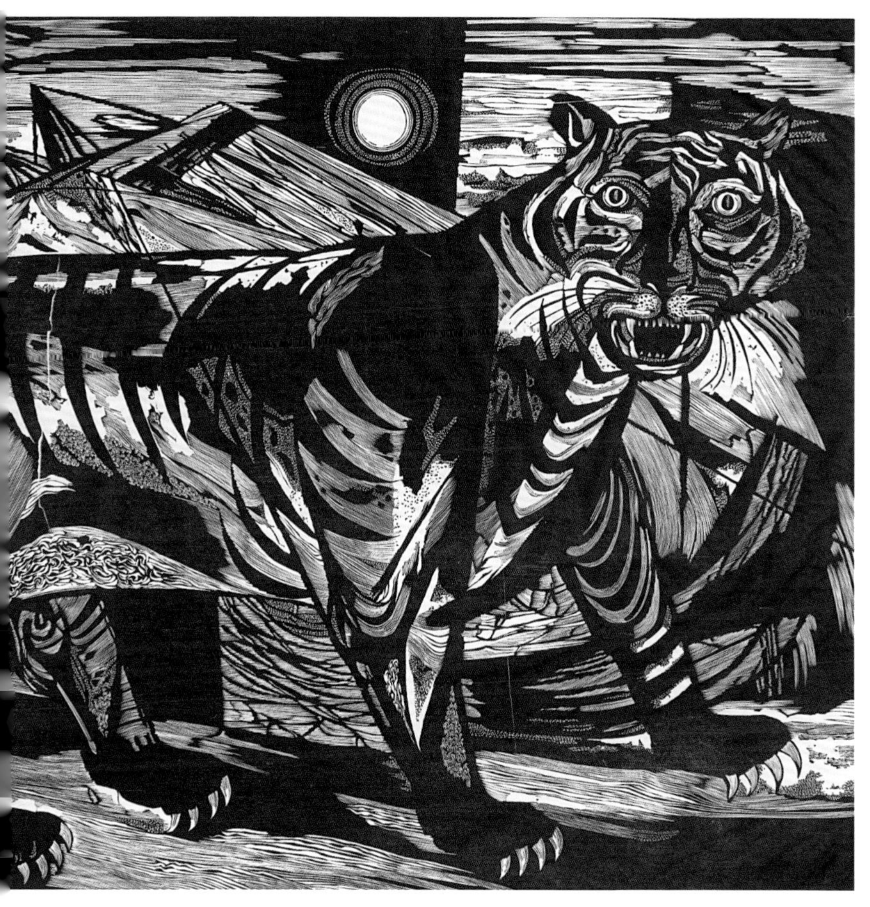

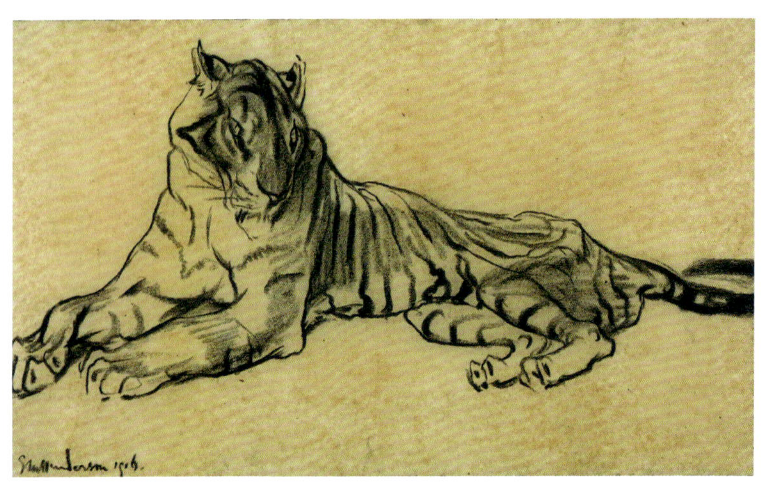

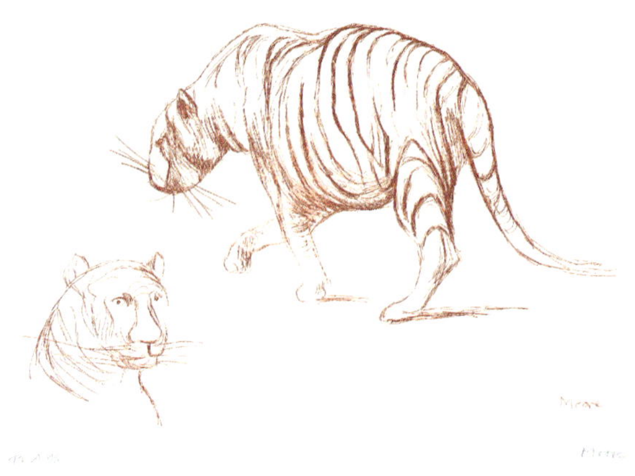

## ELSIE MARIAN HENDERSON

***A Tiger*** 1916

Despite Henderson's modest materials of simply charcoal on paper, there is an inherent elegance to this drawing of a tiger. The curve of powerful paws and supine posture give the impression that this regal feline is indifferent to our presence. Henderson spent her early years as an artist in London, and was commissioned by London Transport to make a poster to promote travel to London Zoo. Many of her early works are of the animals she saw there.

## HENRY MOORE

***Tiger*** 1982

Although regarded as one of the most famous sculptors of the twentieth century, Moore is also recognised as an accomplished draughtsman. To those familiar with his work, this etching carries the unmistakeable hand of the artist. Part of the album entitled *Animals in the Zoo* 1981–2, most of the etchings were made from studying photographs taken by Moore's assistant, Michel Muller. The cat on the left has a dopey expression, making it seem more Tigger than Tiger.

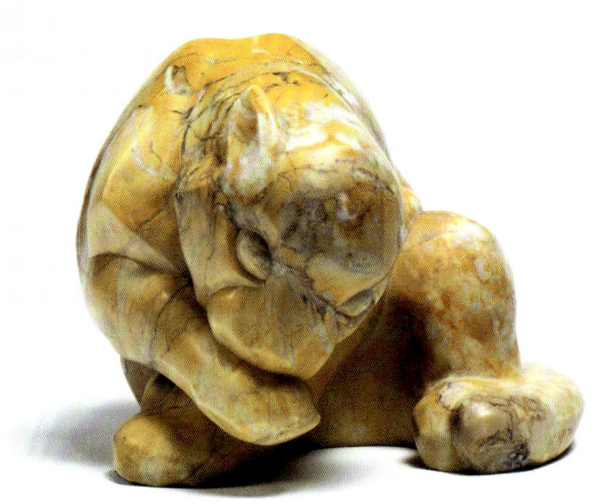

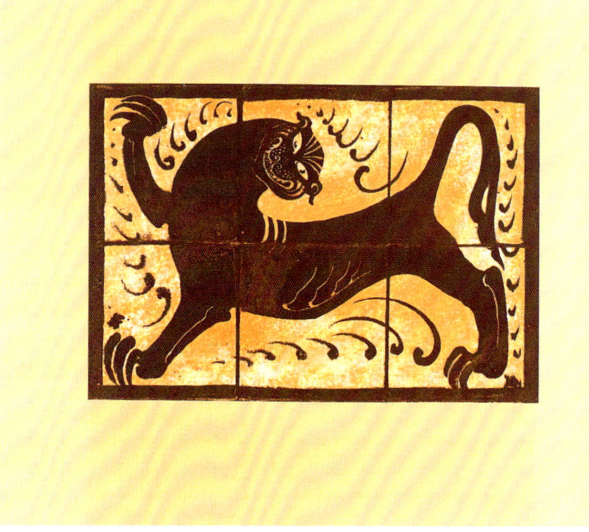

## ALAN L. DURST

*Feline* 1930

Influenced by the direct carving of Auguste Rodin (1840–1917), Durst was interested in the properties of the material he was using and kept his form simple in order to respect the natural colour and textures. Carved directly from Siena marble, this lion-like cat was, according to the artist, the outcome of having a 'very favourite white cat' in his studio, and from his observations of 'her large relations in the zoo'. The cat's pose is one we can all recognise: a feline taking fastidious care over its appearance with self-grooming, a trait characteristic of all cats, big or small.

## BERNARD LEACH

*Lion Tile* 1973–4

Six segments give an impression that this work is composed of ceramic tiles, as one might rightly assume given that this is made by a potter so revered he is often referred to as the 'Father of British studio pottery'. However, the heraldic big cat is in fact a lithograph, reminiscent of the Royal Arms of England: you don't have to go far in the country to stumble upon this rampant attitude emblazoned on flags, football shirts and mugs. The Plantagenets could not have foreseen the heavy and sometimes problematic symbolism the Barbary lion still carries.

## E. BOX

*The Expulsion* 1951

Not one, but two big cats stare resolutely out of the canvas in a naïve style. Despite the painting's title being about the expulsion of Adam and Eve from Paradise, the protagonists here are not humans, but divine animals, pure enough to remain in the Garden of Eden. Animals appear in many of Box's paintings, religious or not, as her hope had always been that there would be a state of co-existence between humans and other living beings: 'We lost that and now beasts are used and abused by man – they have no defences. My feelings simply are love and compassion.'

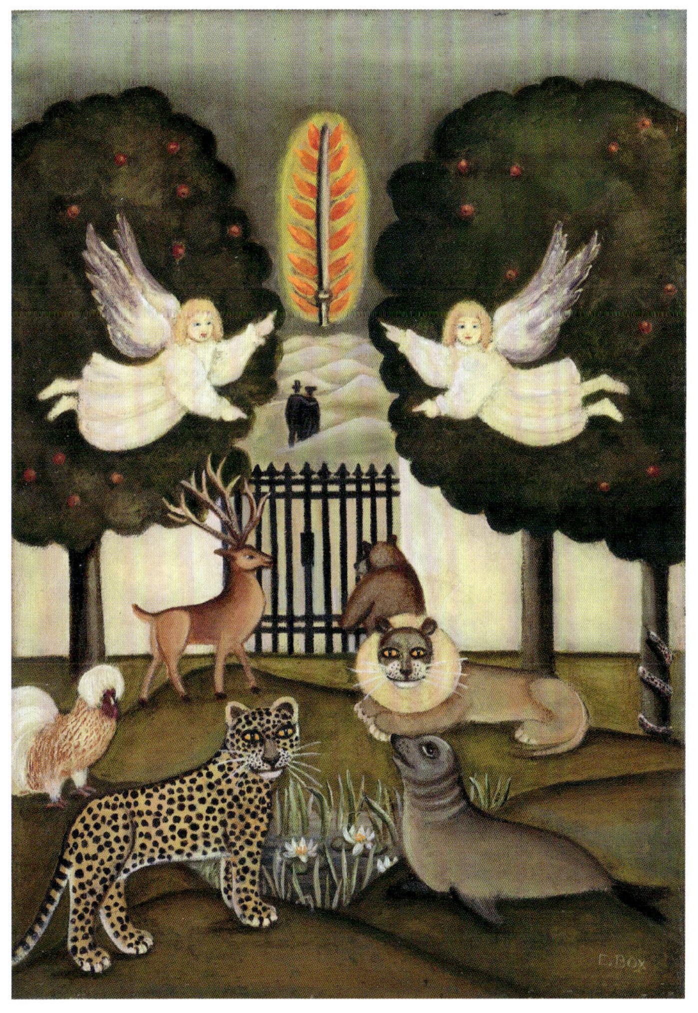

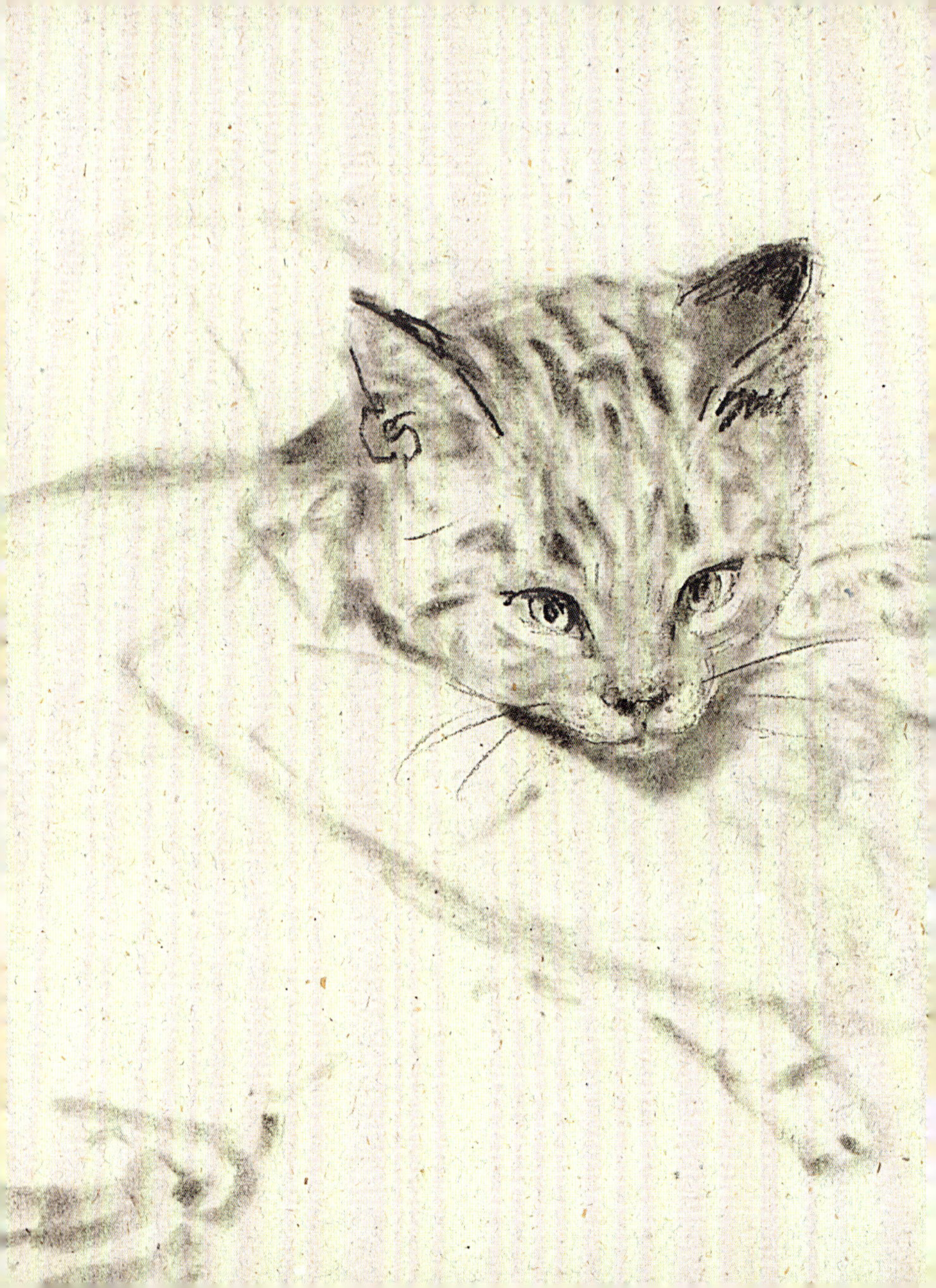

# Scratchy Sketches

Rapidly executed, sketches of cats are intended for the most part to capture the likeness of a cat before it can walk away, indifferent to the ambitions of the artist. Strong-willed, stubborn and easily displeased, cats tend to do as they wish, while we humans do our best to receive attention from them. In some ways the following pencil, chalk, ink and watercolour sketches and studies are the most authentic representations of cats in art. Their single medium allows for a distillation of the essence of the cat to its simplest form – whiskers, ears and paws are caught as temporal moments through a series of lines and scratches on the page.

The sketches are intimate, carried out in domestic and private settings where the cat itself is living, and jotted down into personal sketchbooks documenting the artist's observations and moods. Sometimes the cats are sleeping peacefully; the artist has been honoured with a quiet opportunity to commit the creature to paper, while other times, in the twitch of a whisker the cat has stalked off, fatigued of acting as muse and model.

**JOHN DOWMAN** *A Kitten* n.d.
(detail, see p.66)

## JOHN NASH

*Sketch of a seated woman with cat on her lap* 1920s

Just a quick hashing of lines forms the shapes of this woman, possibly Barbara Nash, the artist's sister, with a cat draped over her lap. John Nash was from an artistic family; his brother Paul was a famous surrealist and war artist, and John himself was a landscape painter and engraver. The Tate archive houses a great many of his writings, letters and sketchbooks, from which this pencil drawing is taken. They offer an insight into his wanderings across the countryside, and into his personal life, where domestic scenes like this take place.

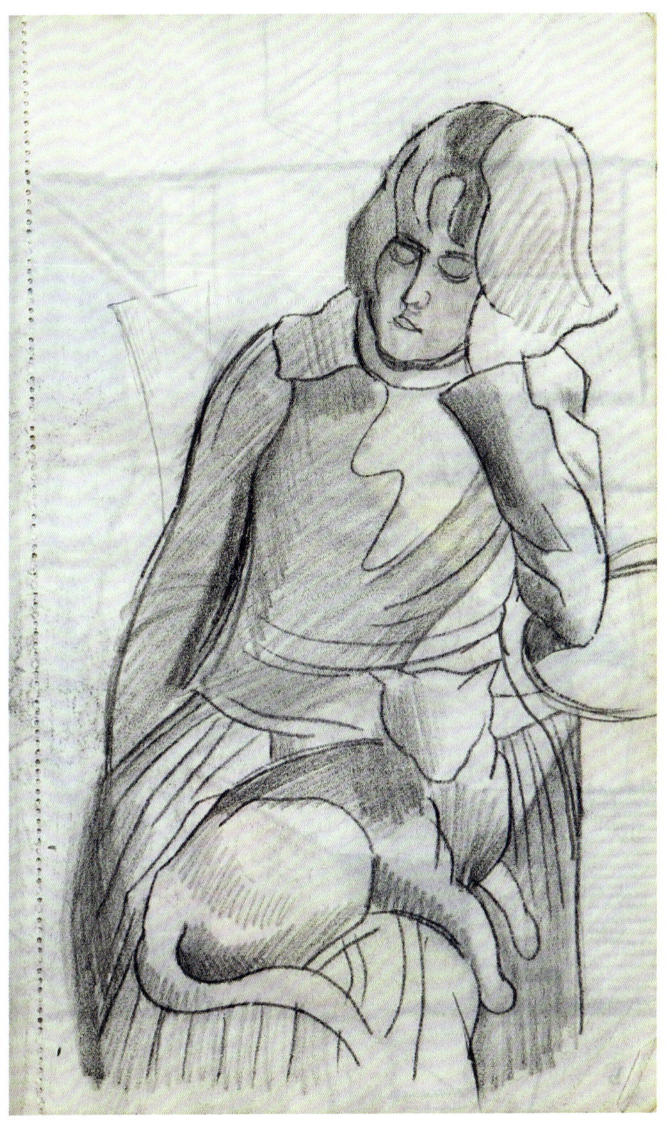

## ANDY WARHOL

*Foot with Cat* 1955–7

There are two recurring themes in Warhol's earlier works: cats and feet. In his commercial work his illustrations are dominated by fashionable shoes, and in his personal drawings he enjoyed depicting feet without their coverings. Warhol would ask friends and lovers to pose as foot models for him, placing carefully chosen objects alongside the bare soles, including roses, beetles, cans of soup and even a lit cigarette between the toes. Here there is a definite erotic languor to what seems to be an impromptu sketch, where a cat is caught poised next to this giant human paw.

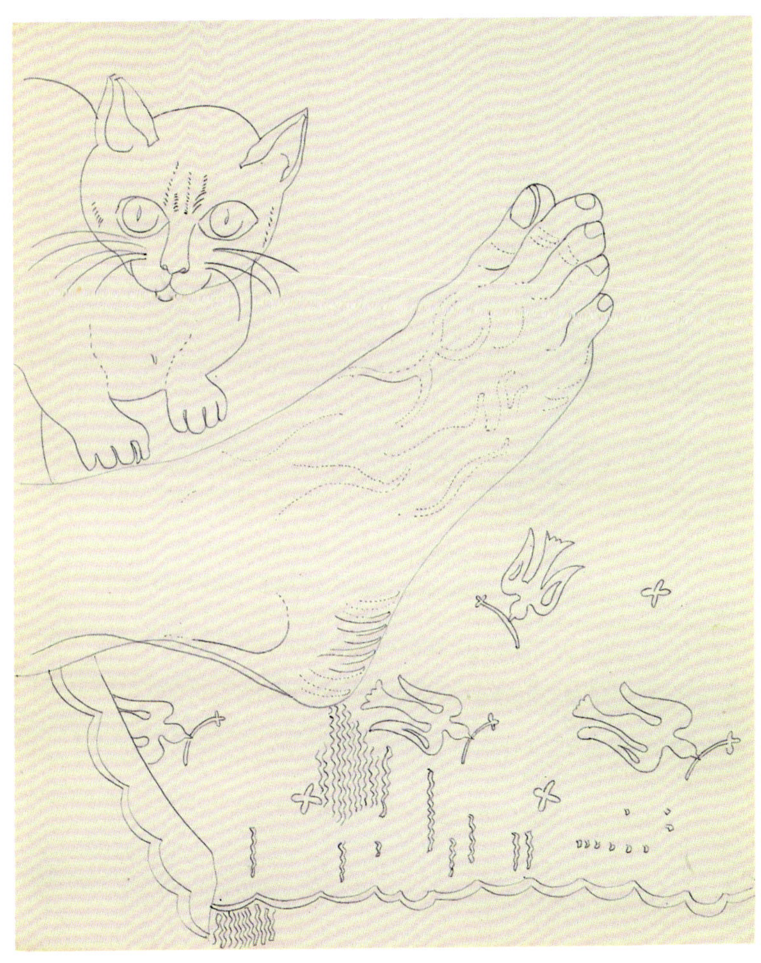

## HENRI GAUDIER-BRZESKA

***Several studies of flowers, a goldfish and a black cat*** 1911

In a sketchbook predominantly of pencil, this ink and watercolour page stands out not just because of its sumptuous colours, but because of the images themselves. Gaudier-Brzeska was an avant-garde sculptor who was deeply concerned with symbolism. The obsidian cat appears to be peering down, perhaps into waters below, where the goldfish swims. The dark purple sheen on both alludes to something more sensual, and the inclusion of the exquisitely detailed orchids adds to a general sense of mystical eroticism.

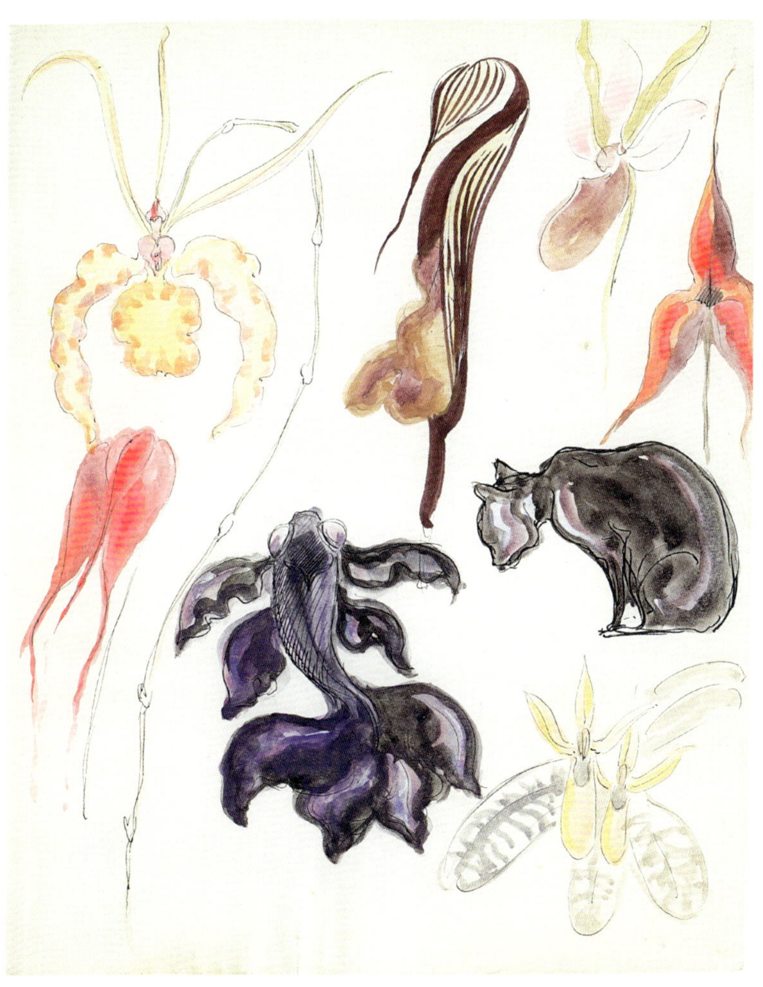

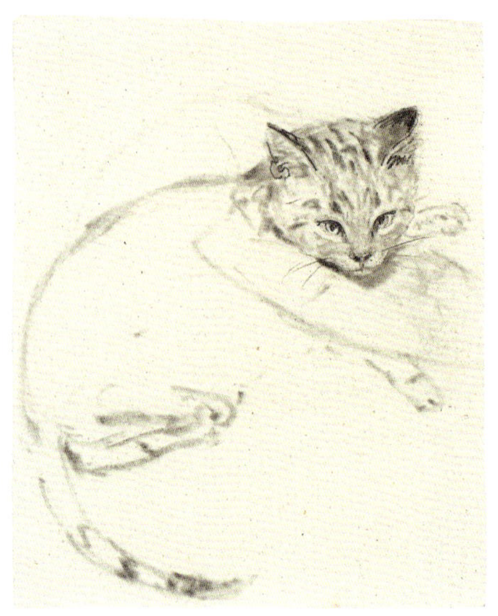

## JOHN DOWNMAN

***A Kitten*** n.d.

One of the most fashionable portraitists of the eighteenth century, Downman's success was thanks to a quick hand in chalk, which allowed him to make several versions of each portrait rapidly. Among his sitters was the Duchess of Devonshire, a name made famous to modern audiences by Kiera Knightley in 2008, and then of course, this obscure little kitten who, although nameless, warranted a sketch. For the sketch Downman used a stump, a tool made of soft leather or paper, for smudging chalk and charcoal.

## J.M.W. TURNER

***Study of a Sleeping Cat*** c.1796–7

Swirling seas, sun-drenched skies, tall ships skimming horizons ... and walking tall among them all ... cats, literally. Perhaps a little-known titbit was that J.M.W. Turner lived with an inordinate amount of Manx cats that belonged to his housekeeper, Hannah Danby. The cats were allowed to roam freely through his studio, sometimes leaving their pawprints across his sketchbooks. It is believed that another Tate work, *Fishing upon the Blythe-Sand, Tide Setting In* 1809 was even used as a cat flap by Danby.

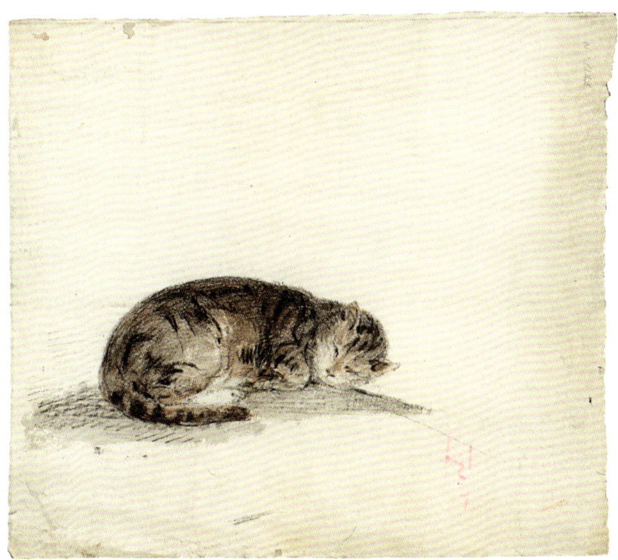

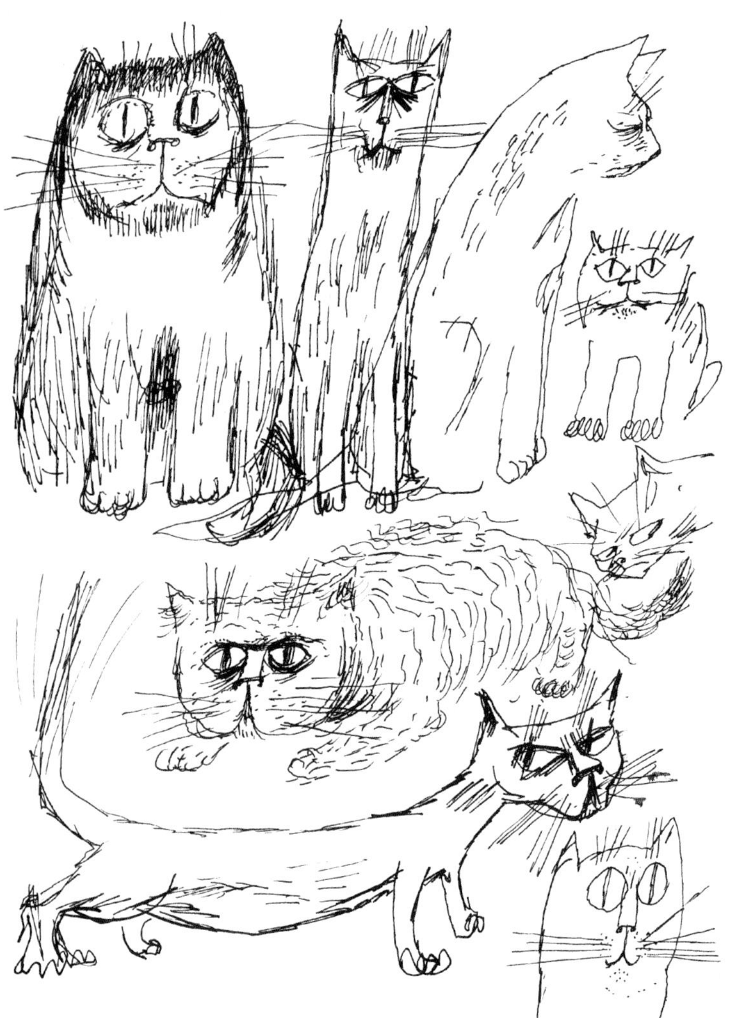

## JAMES BOSWELL

***Study of Eight Cats*** c.1953–4

Bug-eyed cats crowd the page of this sketchbook, their human-like expressions unmistakeable – perplexed, disinterested, cantankerous. The rest of the sketchbook is also full of these crotchety cats, some with paws sullenly folded, others stalking off the page. Communist Boswell was well versed in satirical drawings, having provided prints and cartoons for both the *Left Review* and the *Daily Worker* (now the *Morning Star*), and his informal sketches carry the same dry witticism.

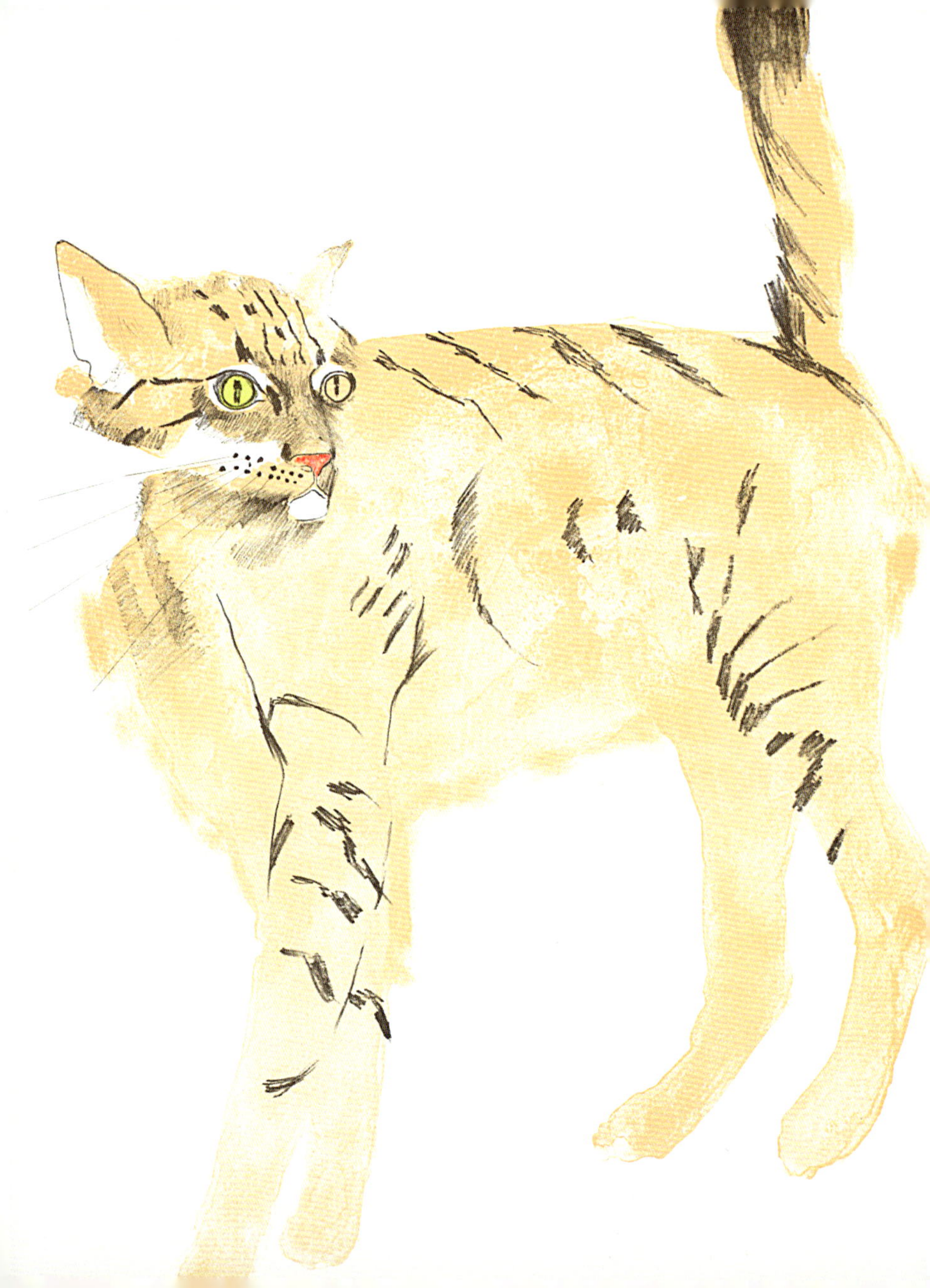

# Prints and Pawings

Scratching and scraping into solid materials is one of the first ways humans created art, using tools to make minuscule engravings on shells or gargantuan geoglyphs in our landscapes, such as the enormous cat recently found in the deserts of Peru, dating back to between 200 and 100 BC. Since then our tools may have changed and evolved, but the instinct to scrape away remains.

The majority of the following cats (and their companions) are stored safely in Tate's Prints and Drawings collection. The vast number and delicate nature of the drawings, watercolours and prints means that only a small collection can be put on display, so these felines live a private life, tucked away in sketchbooks, bestiaries and folios. Bar the beautiful lithograph opposite (produced using the repellence of oil and water), all are examples of intaglio, which refers to printmaking techniques such as etching and engraving, where the image is produced by incising into a printing plate and then filling it with ink and printing it onto paper. The images here include all manner of felines – wild, domestic and big – all executed with pinpoint, scratching precision.

**ELISABETH FRINK** *Wild Cat* 1970
(detail, see p.74)

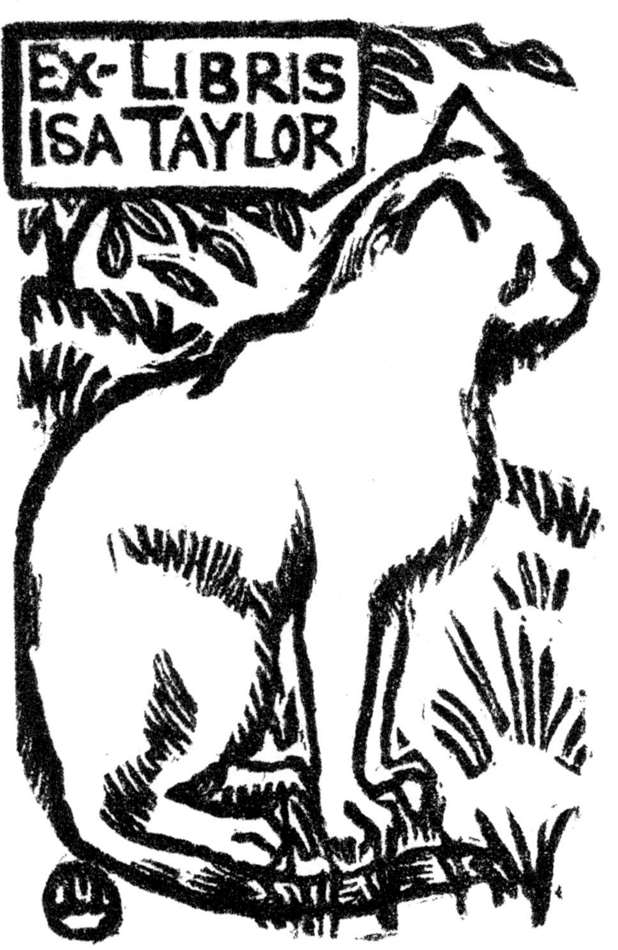
EX-LIBRIS
ISA TAYLOR

## LUCIEN PISSARRO, ESTHER PISSARRO

***Ex Libris Isa Taylor*** c.1892

Esther Pissarro, like her husband, was a wood-engraver and collaborated with him on engraving illustrations for Eragny Press publications, the press they ran together from 1895–1914, which was inspired by William Morris's press. The latin *ex-libris*, meaning 'from the books' is another word for a bookplate, a decorative label that could be pasted into the front of a book to signify its owner. Isa Taylor (later Mrs Cassola) was a dear friend of Esther Pissaro's sister, Ruth, and so this simply hewn but dignified cat would have likely been a gift for her.

## ELISABETH FRINK

*Wild Cat* 1970

Frink is generally known for embodying a postwar consciousness, that of volatile vulnerability. She explored the subtle power-play between prey and predator, and harnessed the human capacity for aggression and suffering within her animal sculptures and prints. In this lithograph the wild cat is on edge; it tiptoes across the page, tail alert, the heterochromia of its eyes highlighting the duality of its life – simultaneously dangerous and endangered.

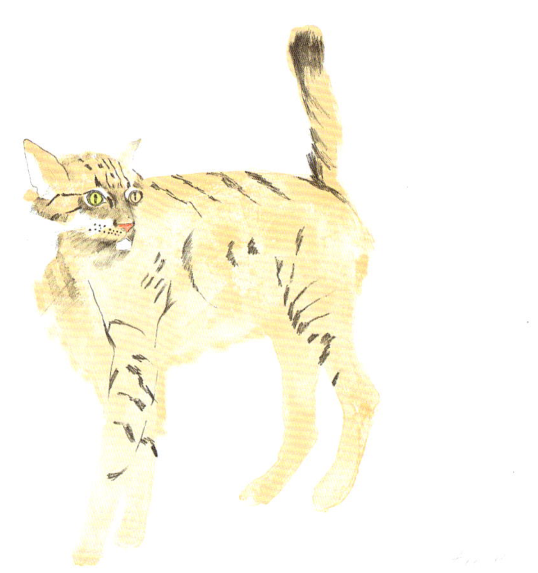

## AFTER FRANCIS BARLOW

***Untitled*** n.d.

Seventeenth-century artist Barlow was Britain's first wildlife painter, inspiring this unknown artist and paving the way for a much-loved tradition that was to find its zenith with George Stubbs's paintings with all their lustrous limbs and flaring nostrils. The motif of a cat and monkey was made popular at the time from *La Fontaine's Fables* (1668) in which a monkey convinced a cat to retrieve hot chestnuts straight from a fire, only to eat them all itself. Whether or not this duo are destined for the same fate, there is definitely a tension between the two, with an odd, cat-like squirrel in the background taking an interest in the proceedings.

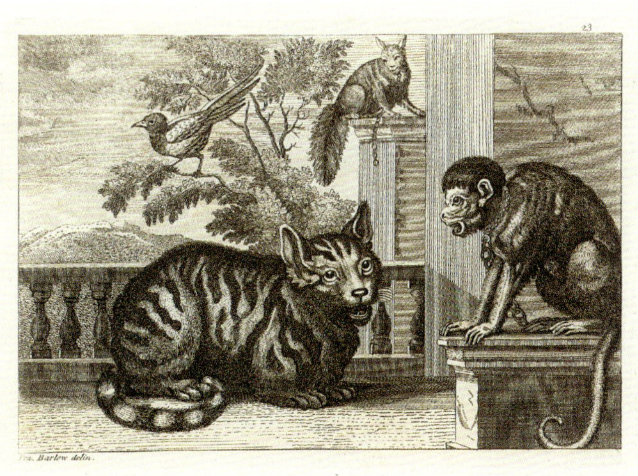

## ARTHUR BOYD HOUGHTON

***My Treasure: Mrs A.B. Houghton and Two Children, engraved by the Dalziel Brothers*** n.d.

Houghton was a popular and prolific Victorian illustrator, contributing to household magazines such as *The Graphic* and *Good Words*. An idealised Pre-Raphaelite scene of pure domestic bliss, the household portrayed here is one of serenity and harmony. The artist's wife is pictured dutifully doting on their two young cherubs, one of whom plays with her hair like a kitten plays with string. The real cat is peacefully sleeping below and signifies the calm and beatific expectation every Victorian husband had of his wife and children.

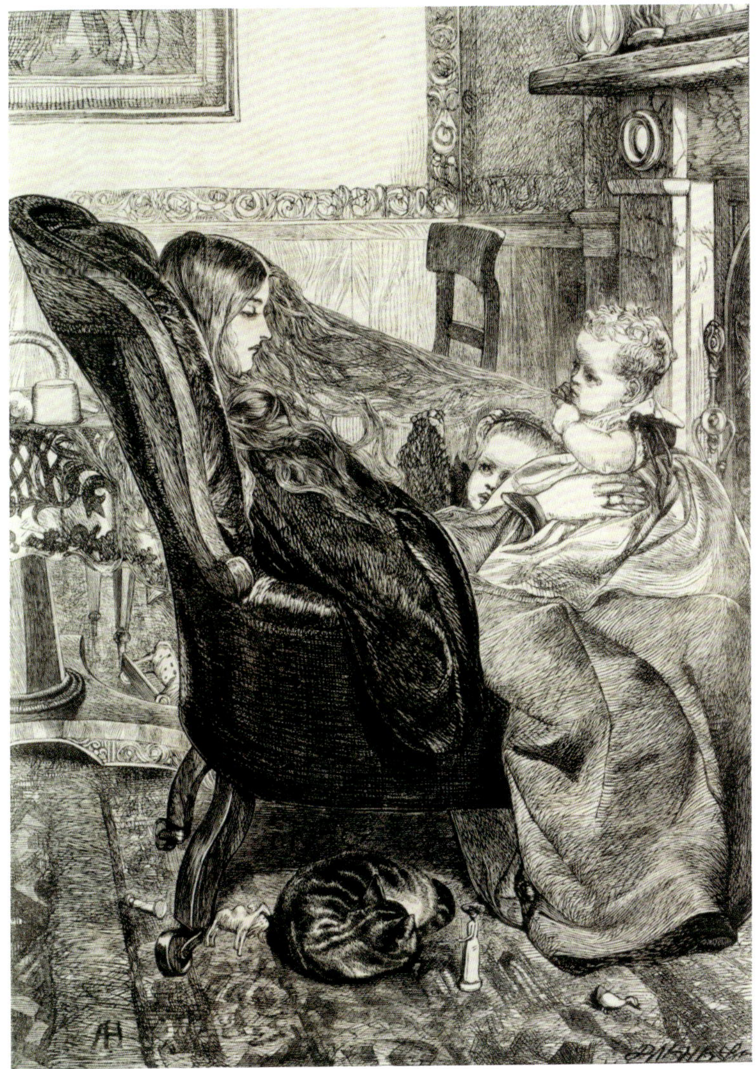

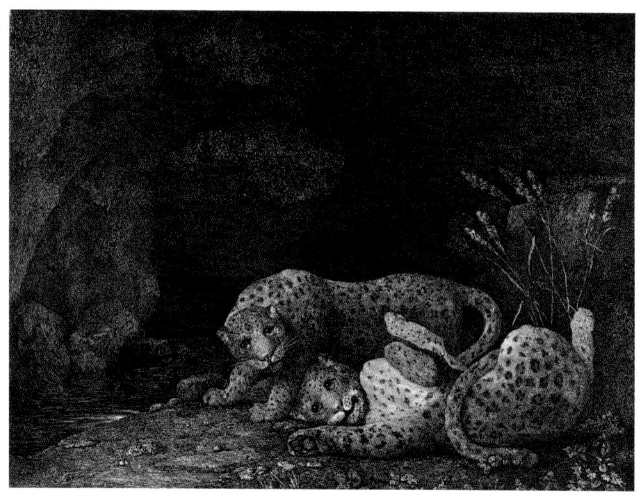

## GEORGE STUBBS

*Leopards at Play* 1780, reprinted 1974

Stubbs, principally renowned for painting horses, a skill born of his study of anatomy, depicts highly detailed renditions of muscles and sinews in his animated works. Somewhat obsessed with the theme of lions attacking horses, he made seventeen paintings across a span of thirty years, all of the same melodrama: the great cats spring on their innocent prey from the darkness, mercilessly plunging their teeth into soft flanks. Here is a more subdued etching of two leopards, who look more like oversized pussycats playing with a ball of string than ferocious wild beasts.

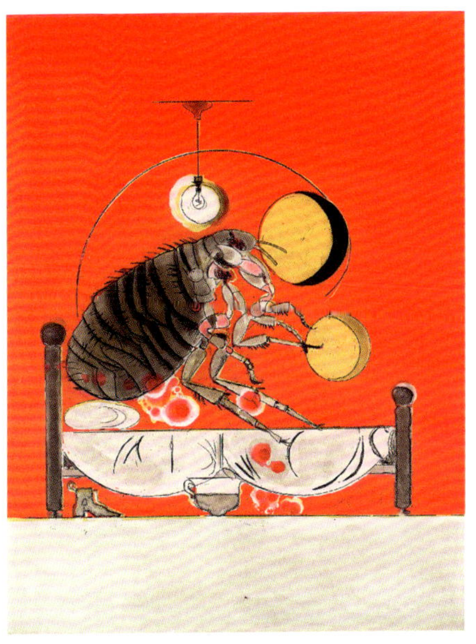

## GRAHAM SUTHERLAND

***The Flea*** 1978–9

This flea is part of the last set of bestiary prints (a compendium of beasts with religious allegorical meaning) which Sutherland made before his death in February 1980. The flea, the original ailurophile – cat lover – is seen here on its bed, highlighting an erotic, almost vampiric behaviour that obsession can bring. The joke was obviously not lost on artist Henri Matisse (1869–1954), who named one of his cats *La Puce*, French for The Flea.

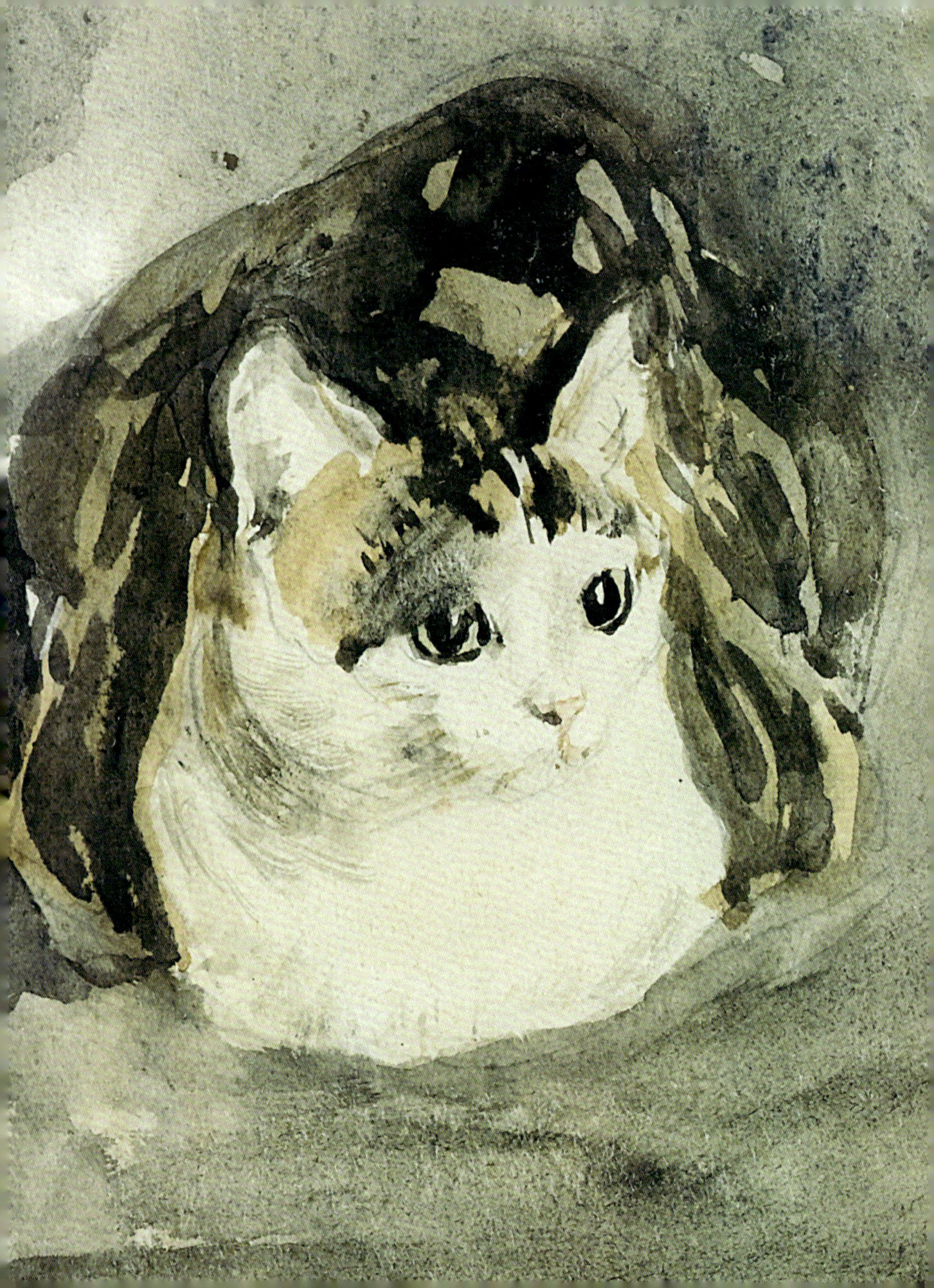

# Painterly Paws

Up until fairly recently in the history of western art, domestic cats have had a mixed treatment. Held in the claws of the religious stereotypes of medieval Christianity, the cat has found it hard to shake off connotations of deceit, desire and betrayal. Domenico Ghirlandaio's fifteenth-century version of the *The Last Supper* even placed a cat purposely behind Judas to signify his treachery. In Europe the cat has by and large been reviled rather than venerated as in other cultures, but gradually the Christian associations diminished and the cat has become accepted as a companion and pet (albeit a somewhat aloof one). The nature of cats – independent, temperamental, enigmatic, docile and dissident – has made them popular pets and subjects for artists, who no doubt were intrigued by their dualistic personality, capable of both sweetness and brutality. Salvador Dalí (1904–89) had his ocelot, Babou – a living accessory to the artist's eccentric character; Ai Wei Wei (b.1957) had around forty cats in his Beijing studio; Gwen John (1876–1939) similarly kept a great many felines as a substitute for the companionship of lovers and friends, and other artists such as Picasso (1881–1973) and Matisse (1869–1954) kept house with their own precious cats. The paintings on the following pages demonstrate that cats will remain forever beguiling and beautiful to artists and cat lovers alike.

**GWEN JOHN** *Cat* c.1904–8
(detail, see p.82)

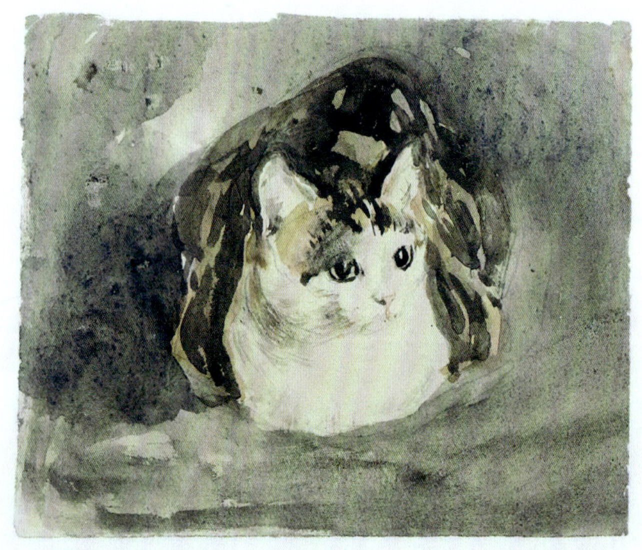

## GWEN JOHN

***Cat*** c.1904–8

Bright-eyed and button-nosed, the tortoiseshell, Edgar Quinet was the apple of her owner's eye and features in most of John's cat drawings. Here the cat's paws are tucked up under her in a contented, sphinx-like pose, but in 1908 she ran away, leaving John in utter dismay. Passionate and obsessive, John wrote a poem about her loss called *Au Chat*, which she sent to artist Auguste Rodin (1840–1917), with whom she was deeply in love but who did not reciprocate.

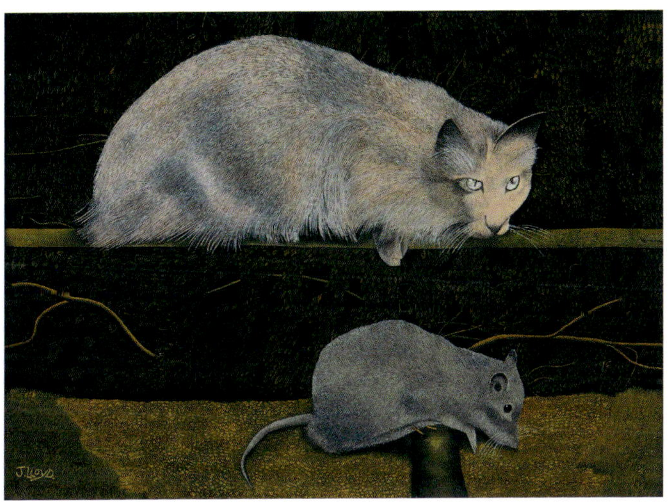


## JAMES LLOYD

*Cat and Mouse* 1967

Yorkshireman James Lloyd, was the first living, self-taught artist to have a painting at Tate, and it was this work here that made it into the gallery. Although inspired by his three white pet cats, this scene is fabricated, and the mouse he said was 'entirely imaginary'. His pointillist style allowed him to fastidiously build up detailed compositions with series of tiny dots and brushstrokes, and it is almost possible to see each individual quivering hair of this cat's glossy flanks as it motionlessly stalks the unsuspecting mouse below; Yorkshire's own Tom and Jerry.

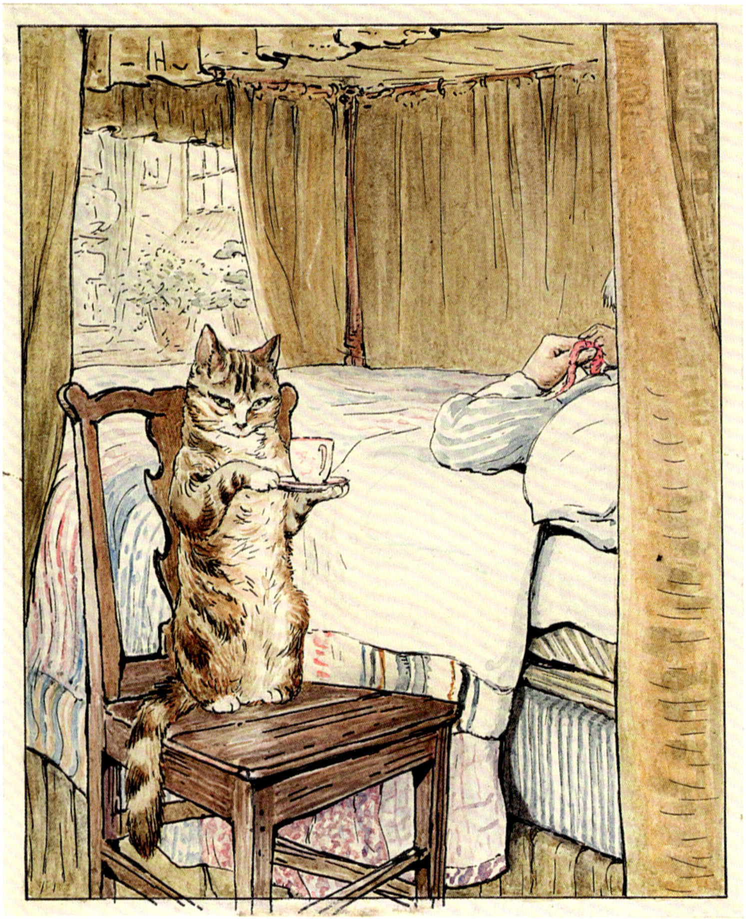

## HELEN BEATRIX POTTER

***Simpkin at the Tailor's Bedside*** c.1902

Tate holds the folios for one of Beatrix Potter's most loved stories, *The Tailor of Gloucester* (1902). Potter was a writer and illustrator as well as a natural scientist and conservationist, and many of her stories are about the intricate imaginary lives of animals. To those unfamiliar with this particular tale, the story centres around one elusive cherry-coloured twist (of silk), which has been hidden by the tailor's mischievous cat, Simpkin after the tailor frees the mice he was intending to eat. This illustration shows bad-tempered Simpkin by the tailor's bedside, after begrudgingly returning the twist.

## MARC CHAGALL

***The Cat Transformed into a Woman*** c.1928–31/1937

In this work Chagall used etching and oil paint to illustrate *La Fontaine's Fables* – classic seventeenth-century tales about morals twisted with an ironic sense of humour. In this particular story, a man adored his pet cat so much that he was able to turn her into a woman and marry her. For a short while he thought his furry kink had resulted in the perfect wife, until he realised she still had a penchant for chasing mice. Chagall's cat-woman seems unimpressed, leaning over the table, one ear pricked, perhaps listening out for her prey.

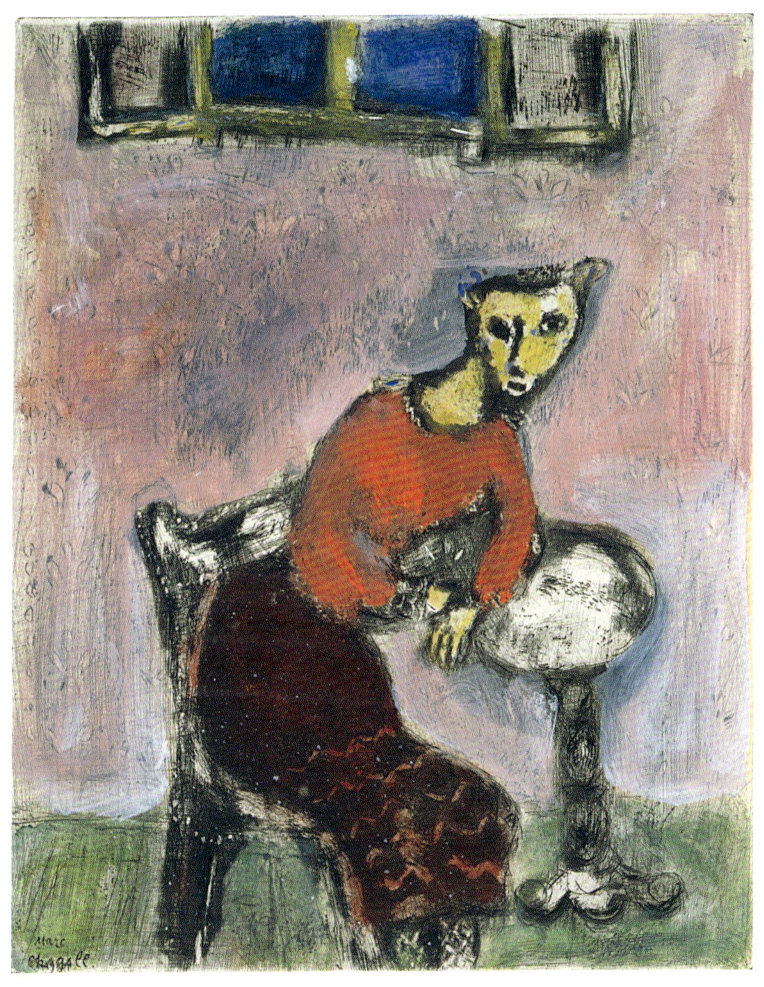
Marc
Chagall

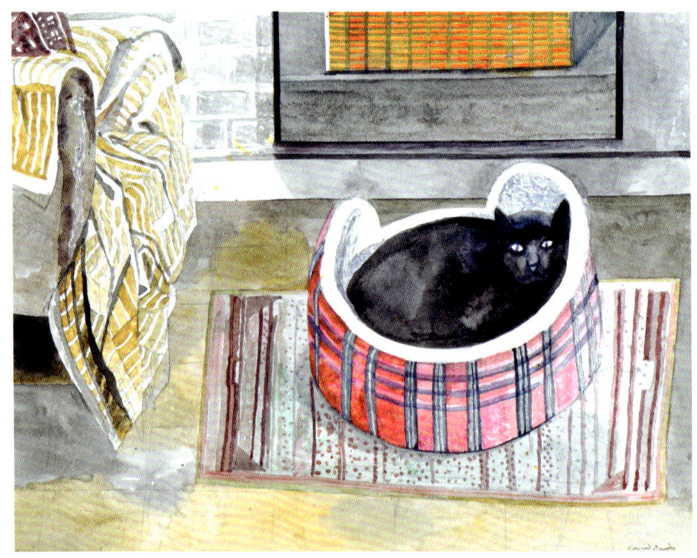

## EDWARD BAWDEN

*Emma Nelson by the Fire* 1987

Edward Bawden was a prolific artist with a varied output, and in his later years he enjoyed painting domestic interiors featuring his cat, Emma Nelson. He often had to draw her first quickly after she had chosen a cosy spot, and then added the background in around her. He once described how Emma Nelson came to him in the spring of 1985 at the Wood Green Animal Shelter, where 'she selected me by jumping up on to my shoulder ... I couldn't have chosen a better feline friend'.

## DUNCAN GRANT

***Girl at the Piano*** 1940

This Hammershøi-like composition restricts the viewer's eye. We are given carefully controlled access through reflections in mirrors and views through windows, the protagonists unwilling to communicate, with a turned back and a sleeping cat. The house is of course the celebrated Charleston, the Sussex farmhouse of the Bloomsbury Group. The girl with her back to us is the illegitimate daughter of Duncan Grant (1885–1978) and Vanessa Bell (1879–1961), who up until the age of seventeen thought she was the daughter of her mother's husband, Clive Bell. The tangled relationships of the group, intimated by the closed composition of this painting, she would later detail in a frank memoir.

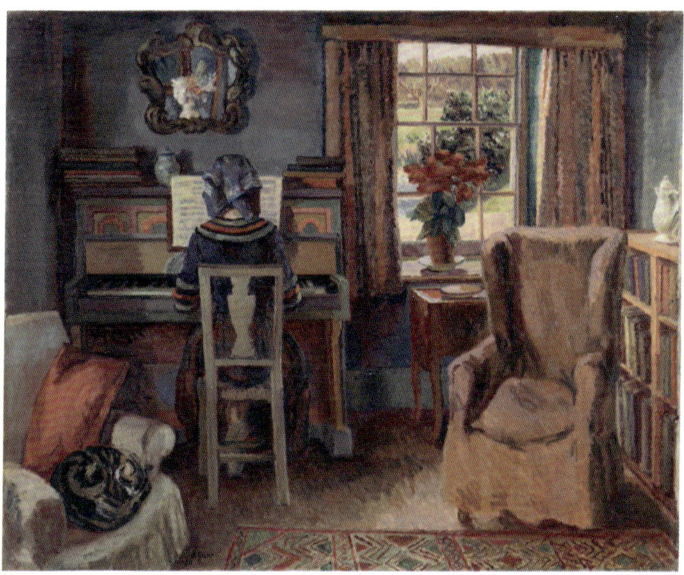

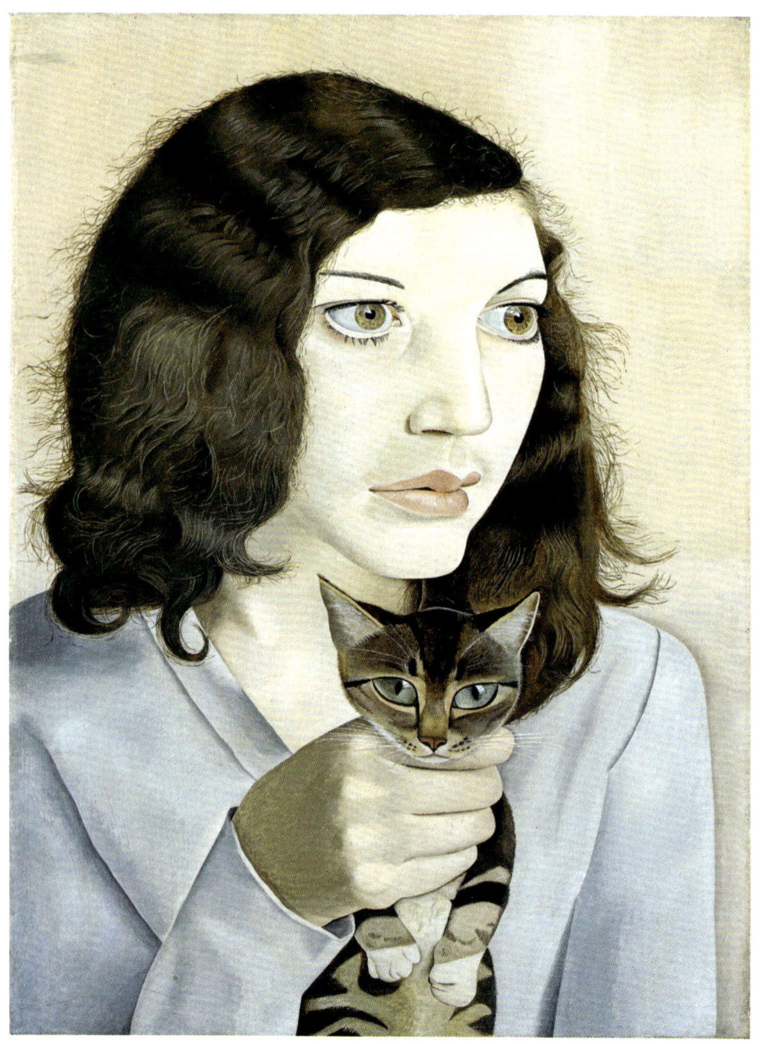

## LUCIAN FREUD

***Girl with a Kitten*** 1947

Two impenetrable gazes. daughter of Jacob Epstein, Kathleen Garman (whose nickname was Kitty) holds a kitten tightly between white knuckles. Kathleen was Freud's first but not last wife, and one cannot help but try and read between the lines in this image. This was one of eight portraits Freud made of her between 1947 and 1951, and in each the same precision of brushwork is executed using fine sable brushes. The needle-sharp style evokes a strand of realist painting, New Objectivity, which started in Germany in the 1920s.

## JOHN RUSSELL

***Boy and Cat*** 1791

At first glance this neoclassical image appears to be an oil painting, but it is in fact a work in pastel, a medium that eighteenth-century artist John Russell most frequently employed. He achieved his characteristic blurring effect by smudging the pastel with his finger and then adding finishing details in black, which can be seen here on the tabby's fur coat. The mincing looks, satin bows and silky paws suggest a hangover of rococo frivolity. Russell was also an astronomer, and produced many studies of the moon after studying it for twenty years; the deep blue sky in the background perhaps alludes to his night-time pastel projects.

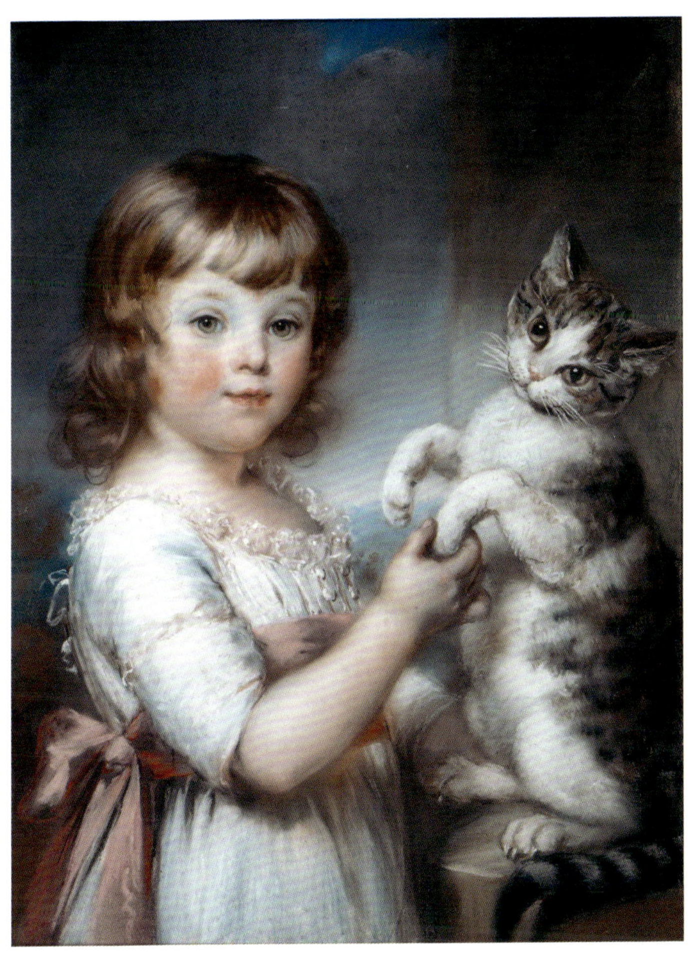

# ILLUSTRATED WORKS

Measurements of artworks are given in centimetres, height before width and depth

**UNKNOWN ARTIST**
*Black and white photograph of Ian Breakwell's 'Circus' a photo-silkscreen collage featuring the heads of a cat, lion, tiger, warthog and giraffe above a circus ring* 1978
Black and white photograph
30.4 x 21.6
p.43

**EILEEN AGAR 1899–1991**
*Photograph of Bella the cat lying down* c.1936
Black and white photograph
6.4 x 6.6
p.33

**AFTER FRANCIS BARLOW 1626–1704**
*Untitled* n.d.
Part of *Various Birds and Beasts Drawn from the Life*
Engraving and etching on paper
12.5 x 18.8
p.75

**EDWARD BAWDEN 1903–89**
*Emma Nelson by the Fire* 1987
Graphite and watercolour on paper
49.8 x 64.5
p.88

**JAMES BOSWELL 1906–71**
*Study of Eight Cats* c.1953–4
Ink, crayon, graphite and watercolour on paper. From a sketchbook
25.5 x 20.3
p.68

**E. BOX 1919–88**
*The Expulsion* 1951
Oil paint and acrylic paint on canvas
50.2 x 36.2
p.57

**MARC CHAGALL 1887–1985**
*The Cat Transformed into a Woman* c.1928–31/1937
Etching, drypoint and oil paint on paper
29.5 x 24.1
p.87

**PRUNELLA CLOUGH 1919–99**
*Black and white photograph of a cat winding itself around a man's legs* 1950s
Black and white photograph
8 x 10.5
p.29

*Colour photograph of a cat in a window* 1986
Colour photograph
10.1 x 13
p.29

**BRUCE DAVIDSON b.1933**
*Girl holding kitten* 1960
Gelatin silver print on paper
46 x 30.8
p.35

**JOHN DOWNMAN 1750–1824**
*A Kitten* n.d.
Chalk on paper
22.9 x 19
pp.58 (detail), 66

**ALAN L. DURST 1883–1970**
*Feline* 1930
Siena marble
19 x 26.7 x 21
p.54

**LUCIAN FREUD 1922–2011**
*Girl with a Kitten* 1947
Oil paint on canvas
41 x 30.7
p.90

**ELISABETH FRINK 1930–93**
*Wild Cat* 1970
Part of *Wild Animals* 1970
Lithograph on paper
51.9 x 66
pp.70 (detail), 74

**HENRI GAUDIER-BRZESKA 1891–1915**
*Several studies of flowers, a goldfish and a black cat* 1911
Graphite, ink and watercolour on paper. From a sketchbook, 35 pages and 3 loose leaves plus covers
25.6 x 21.8
p.65

**DUNCAN GRANT 1885–1978**
*Girl at the Piano* 1940
Oil paint on canvas
117.5 x 147.3
pp.4–5 (detail), 89

**SUNIL GUPTA b.1953**
*Roger & Steve, London* 1984, printed 2018
Inkjet on paper
50 x 33
pp.8 (detail), 18

**ELSIE MARIAN HENDERSON 1880–1967**
*A Tiger* 1916
Charcoal on paper
21.6 x 36.2
p.52

**NIGEL HENDERSON 1917–85**
*Photograph of an unidentified girl holding a Siamese cat* c.1949–56
Black and white photograph
5.5 x 5.5
p.25

**DAVID HOCKNEY b.1937**
*Mr and Mrs Clark and Percy* 1970–1
Acrylic paint on canvas
213.4 x 304.8
p.13

**ARTHUR BOYD HOUGHTON 1836–75**
*My Treasure: Mrs A.B. Houghton and Two Children, engraved by the Dalziel Brothers* n.d.
Woodcut on paper
16.5 x 12.1
p.77

**GWEN JOHN 1876–1939**
*Cat* c.1904–8
Graphite and watercolour on paper
11.1 x 13.7
pp.80 (detail), 82

*Young Woman Holding a Black Cat* c.1920–5
Oil paint on canvas
46 x 29.8
p.23

**MISCH KOHN 1916–2002**
*Tiger* c.1949
Print on paper
41.6 x 60.6
pp.50–1

**EDWIN HENRY LANDSEER 1802–73**
*Study of a Lion* c.1862
Oil paint on canvas
91.4 x 137.8
pp.46–7

**BERNARD LEACH 1887–1979**
*Lion Tile* 1973–4
Lithograph on paper
43.5 x 52.1
p.54

**JOHN FREDERICK LEWIS 1805–76**
*Head of a Lion* 1824
Watercolour on paper
34.3 x 26
p.49

**RICHARD LINDNER 1901–78**
*Homage to a Cat* 1952
Oil paint on canvas
92.1 x 60.3
p.11

**JAMES LLOYD 1905–74**
*Cat and Mouse* 1967
Gouache on board
38.1 x 53.3
p.83

**EDOUARD MANET 1832–83**
*Woman with a Cat* c.1880
Oil paint on canvas
92.1 x 73
p.14

**HENRY MOORE 1898–1986**
*Tiger* 1982
Etching on paper
27.3 x 35.2
p.52

**DAIDO MORIYAMA b.1938**
*Memory* 2012
Gelatin silver print on paper
150 x 100
p.36

**JOHN NASH 1893–1977**
*Sketch of a seated woman with a cat on her lap* 1920s
Graphite and watercolour on paper. From a sketchbook, 22 pages plus cover
20.2 x 13
p.61

*Window Plants* 1945
Lithograph on paper
49.8 x 76.2
p.17

**PETER PHILLIPS b.1939**
*Six Times Eight, Dreaming* 1974
Lithograph on paper
61 x 79.7
p.30

**LUCIEN PISSARRO 1863–1944**
**ESTHER PISSARRO 1870–1951**
*Ex Libris Isa Taylor* c.1892
Woodcut on paper
5.7 x 3.8
p.72

**JOHN RUSSELL 1744–1807**
*Boy and Cat* 1791
Pastel on paper
58.7 x 44.5
p.93

**HELEN BEATRIX POTTER 1866–1943**
*Simpkin at the Tailor's Bedside* c.1902
Part of illustrations for *The Tailor of Gloucester*
Ink, watercolour and gouache on paper
11.1 x 9.2
p.84

**STEPHEN SHORE b.1947**
*Canyon, Texas, July 1972* 1972, printed 2006
Part of *American Surfaces* 1972–3
Digital C-print on paper
12.7 x 19
pp.26 (detail), 31

**GEORGE STUBBS 1724–1806**
*Leopards at Play* 1780, reprinted 1974
Etching and engraving on paper
35.6 x 46.7
p.78

*A Lion Resting on a Rock* published 1788
Engraving on paper
22.7 x 31.4
p.40

**GRAHAM SUTHERLAND 1903–80**
*The Flea* 1978–9
Part of *The Bestiary or the Procession of Orpheus*
Etching and aquatint on paper
47.2 x 36.3
p.79

**J.M.W. TURNER 1775–1851**
*Cottage Interior by Firelight*
1790–1
Part of *Oxford and Other Subjects*
Graphite and watercolour on paper
25.4 x 33.1
p.16

*Study of a Sleeping Cat*
c.1796–7
Part of *Figure Studies*
Chalk and watercolour on paper
23.8 x 27.8
p.67

**FELICITAS VOGLER 1922–2006**
*Photograph of Ben Nicholson holding his cat, Tommy* 1968
Black and white photograph
12.5 x 11.3
p.33, cover

**ETHEL WALKER 1861–1951**
*The Hon. Mrs Adams* c.1901
Oil paint on canvas
90.2 x 74.3
p.21

**ANDY WARHOL 1928–87**
*Foot with Cat* 1955–7
Ink on paper
42.4 x 35
p.63

*Siberian Tiger* 1983
Part of *Endangered Species* 1983
Screenprint on board
96.5 x 96.5
pp.38 (detail), 41

**KARL WESCHKE 1925–2005**
*Tiger Tiger* 1953
Woodcut on paper
45.5 x 30
p.45

# CREDITS

COPYRIGHT
© The Estate of Edward Bawden 88

© James Boswell Archive 68

© Estate of Eden Box. All Rights Reserved, DACS 2020 57

© The Estate of Ian Breakwell. All rights reserved. DACS 2021 43

Marc Chagall © ADAGP, Paris and DACS, London 2021 87

© Bruce Davidson/Magnum Photos 35

© Estate of Alan L. Durst 54 top

© Fondation du Refuge SPA de Saint-Légier-la-Chiésaz cover, 33 bottom

© The Lucian Freud Archive / Bridgeman Images 90

© The Elisabeth Frink Estate and Archive. All Rights Reserved, DACS 2021 70, 74

© J. Henderson 52 top

© Nigel Henderson Estate 25

© David Hockney. Collection Tate, U.K. 12–13

© Sunil Gupta. All rights reserved, DACS 2021 8, 18

© Estate of Misch Kohn 50–1

© The Bernard Leach Family. All rights reserved, DACS 2021 54 bottom

Richard Lindner © ADAGP, Paris and DACS, London 2021 11

© Nancy Ann Lloyd 83

Reproduced by permission of The Henry Moore Foundation 52 bottom

© Daido Moriyama Photo Foundation 36

© The John Nash Estate / Bridgeman Images 17, 61

© Peter Phillips. All Rights Reserved, DACS 2021 30

© The estate of Ann Robin-Banks 29

© Stephen Shore. Courtesy 303 Gallery, New York 26, 31

© The estate of Graham Sutherland 79

© Tate, 2021 33 top, 89

© 2021 The Andy Warhol Foundation for the Visual Arts, Inc. / Licensed by DACS, London 63

© 2021 The Andy Warhol Foundation for the Visual Arts, Inc. / Licensed by DACS, London / Ronald Feldman Gallery, New York 38, 41

© The Estate of Karl Weschke. All rights reserved, DACS 2021 45

PHOTOGRAPHY
©Tate, 2021 cover, 4–5, 8, 11, 12–13, 14, 16, 17, 18, 23, 25, 26, 29, 30, 31, 33, 35, 36, 38, 40, 41, 43, 45, 46–7, 49, 50–1, 52, 54, 58, 61, 63, 65, 66, 67, 68, 70, 72, 74, 75, 77, 78, 79, 80, 82, 83, 84, 87, 88, 89, 90, 93; / Andrew Dunkley 21, 57, 93